Seagram's

COMPLETE
PARTY GUIDE

*invites you
to have fun at your own party*

Learn how to make the power of positive planning work for you. Sylvia Schur guides you expertly and efficiently so that you can give a party and have as much fun as your guests.
She helps you:

- Plan your party, select your menu, arrange your space and invite your guests.

- Schedule your advance preparation and buy your supplies selectively, amply and thriftily.

- Choose the spirits, set up the bar and adapt bartender techniques for easier home serving.

- Set your table or buffet for a few or for many guests—for cocktails, dinner or dessert.

- Prepare delectable dishes, memorable drinks.

- Plan for parties outside your home.

WITH SEAGRAM'S COMPLETE PARTY GUIDE
you can give the best parties ever!

And, as Sylvia Schur reminds you,
"The best part of your own party is that you can't predict what the best part will be."

Seagram's COMPLETE PARTY GUIDE

How to Succeed at Party Planning, Drink Mixing, the Art of Hospitality

by Sylvia Schur

WARNER BOOKS

A Warner Communications Company

To All Those Who Enjoy People
Enough To Plan a Party . . .

Cover and Photographs by Arthur Beck

Interior Illustrations by Howard R. Roberts

Book design by Helen Roberts

Warner Books, Inc., 75 Rockefeller Plaza,
New York, N.Y. 10019

Ⓦ A Warner Communications Company

Printed in the United States of America

First Printing: June, 1979

10   9   8   7   6   5   4

Contents

About Seagram

Seagram is proud to produce the finest distilled products sold in America . . . to satisfy the tastes of discriminating consumers who serve liquor as part of other pleasures. Recognizing that today's consumer wants to combine casual modes of entertaining with professional approaches for food and drink preparation, this book is designed to serve today's varied lifestyles and distinctive tastes.

About The Author

Sylvia Schur is a leading American food editor and journalist. The author of 12 cookbooks and hundreds of magazine and newspaper articles on entertaining, including guides to effective drink mixing and the creative use of liqueurs as flavoring agents. A distinguished hostess, both at home and professionally, she has worked as a consultant, planning menus and bar specialties for famous restaurants and special events. She is food editor of Parade, and heads Creative Food Service, Inc., a food testing and development group.

PART 1

*Welcome to
the Good Life*

1

"Come on Over — I'm Having a Party!"

Say it to one friend.

Or say it to a whole bunch of friends.

Either way, you're having a party . . . and you can enjoy the event as much as your guests!

THE PARTY KNACK . . . OR IS IT KNOW-HOW?

The best parties just seem to happen. Some people have the party knack . . . or is it know-how?

We at Seagram's think that more than knack, or know-how, it's *you!* Party-giving should reflect your own personality. The drinks you mix, the food you prepare, and the way you serve it—whether a snack, a buffet, or a complete dinner—have your own individual stamp. Your guests will exclaim, "Only *you* could have given this terrific party this way!"

WELCOME TO THE GOOD LIFE

We've polled famous hosts and hostesses, bartenders and restaurateurs, working couples and singles, to make *Seagram's Complete Party Guide* easy for you to use. You will find tips for party-readiness, recipes for more than two hundred drinks, bartender tips for successful mixing, ideas for decorations—and preparing your home for a really big party. More than anything else, you will find the power of positive planning, to say "Come over to my house" and mean it.

"ANY DAY" IS A GOOD THEME FOR A PARTY

If it's very cold, offer warming drinks; if it's hot out, stir up your favorite coolers. From New Year's Day through February Valentine's, March St. Patrick's, April Easter brunch, May showers, June receptions, July barbecues, August picnics, September welcomes, October Halloween parties, November Thanksgiving and Big Game get-togethers, December Christmas, anniversaries, birthdays—and 364 unbirthdays—the year is a calendar of events you can make special.

A PARTY BRINGS PEOPLE TOGETHER

In small homes or large, hospitality needs a starting point: *you.* Wanting to bring people together, with a plan for hospitality. Your "bar" may be built-in or a converted basket; your table elaborate or a cloth over an ironing board . . . but it is your cordial welcome that makes your home a fun place. You will enjoy the glow that comes of knowing your friends look forward to your parties. A party planner is always popular.

SALUTE TO YOUR GUESTS' TASTES

When planning a party, think in terms of what your guests like, the combinations of people, and the foods and drinks that make the menu. It's good to have old friends get together, and more interesting to spice a familiar mixture of people with some new personalities. Just be sure that each guest has someone of like tastes or interests with whom to talk. And plan food and drink to satisfy the appetites of your visitors.

PARTIES PLANNED AND SPONTANEOUS

It's best to begin thinking about a planned party a month in advance, and invite your friends, in writing or over the phone, two weeks or more ahead, to allow time for fitting your party into their plans. But if you find that you are in the mood to entertain, and equipped to do so, "Come on over tonight" or "Come for brunch tomorrow" may be a very welcome invitation. The times of parties are as flexible now as today's techniques of entertaining. For sports fans, and for working families, weekend brunch may provide an ideal time to get together, to share game-watching as part of the party. For some families, a big cocktail party is a great way to get a large group of friends together or gather the neighbors for an "open house." This may be an even better party if guests stay on and it grows into a cocktail supper, easily served with a few main dishes and salads set out buffet style.

A sit-down dinner party calls for more planning. Or your crowd may prefer to get together later in the evening, for after-dinner drinks, dessert, and coffee. Whichever kind of party you plan, let guests know both time and type of menu so they can enjoy your party fully.

HOSPITALITY ON HAND

Your first key to ready hospitality is an always-ready plan for something to serve should guests stop in. The key for one famous hostess was just that—a key to turn open a can of paté, served on freshly made toast, with a drink. You may keep a reserve can of nuts, corn to pop, a package of chips or pretzels, or a long-keeping cheese, or prepare some hot herbed bread, while you set out glasses for a welcoming drink.

"B. Y. O." IS IN STYLE

If you know the larder is low, guests may enjoy the party even more if you say, "I'd love to have you come over—

please bring your own. . . ." Pot-luck suppers are the "in" solution to little-time, no-help parties, and a bottle may be the easiest thing for no-cook guests to bring.

If a number of guests are sharing in the party plan, it doesn't hurt to share some hints as to type of food or drink, so that there is good variety for all. "Would you rather bring a casserole or a dessert? I'll make the other." Or, "We have Seagram's V.O., and Mary is bringing a bottle of Myers's Rum. Would it be easy for you to bring Seagram's Extra Dry Gin, so we can try that Red Baron you like so much—or Wolfschmidt Vodka? If not, don't give it a second thought. Just bring you." Give your guest a choice, not a chore.

"PLACING" THE PARTY

People are the most important party ingredient in your party mix. From the first welcome, you want your guests to feel you've planned for their comfort. Show them where to put their belongings, or hang up coats for them. If there are newcomers to the group, introduce them to at least a few of the other guests, along with clues to their interests. And even if guests have met before, it doesn't hurt to bring them up-to-date about each other. It's easier for guests to entertain each other when they have a re-established bond. Set up a spot to serve as your bar, and another area for food—then direct guests to what is available.

MAKING THE MOST OF SPACE

Think about the space available to you before you plan a big party. If you live in a small apartment, you may find that pushing back the furniture or even stripping your living room (store some pieces with a friendly neighbor) is the best bet for a large cocktail party. Even in most small apartments, you can entertain up to twenty at a stand-up cocktail party—with some folding chairs available for tired-feet guests. Or plan a series of smaller dinners, for more of a chance to talk with your friends.

PARTIES "BACK-TO-BACK"

Many good party-givers plan on parties "back-to-back," because two parties can be given with little extra work in preparation and with economy in buying and in effort. The same flowers and candles serve for two occasions, and many of the same foods can be offered. An ingenious hostess serves a whole turkey at dinner party one, carving just one side. The next evening, the same turkey, cut side down, is regally regarnished. And for the third party, the remainder is served as a sliced-turkey platter or turkey curry, or with spaghetti sauce, salad.

THE MOST FOR YOUR MONEY

Even with careful buying and advance planning, party costs can run up! Here is where your ingenuity in balance comes in. An inexpensive menu, even a soup supper, can register you as the smart cook of the crowd and allow budget for the quality drinks you want to offer. A tray of home-made chips, or an unusual vegetable cut into sticks and passed with a flavorful spread, can be more interesting, at far less cost, than expensive but more ordinary hors d'oeuvre.

THE PARTY FOR YOUR OCCASION

If you feel you have met a number of people casually and would like to know them better, a series of small dinner parties will help you achieve that goal. You may plan one superb menu, even prepare and freeze some of the dishes ahead, in quantity. Then invite guests in groups of six and eight, so that you all have a chance to get to know each other better. No need to change the menu while you continue to change the guests!

Part of planning the party is selecting the guests who will "go together." Set off the conversational spark-makers, then let the guests discover each other—and you.

Plan the table settings to match the mood of the occasion—and again, this may be more a matter of taste than of money. If you set a large table and your table top is pristine glass or gleaming wood, let them show. If you are improvising a tabletop, whether with a folding top or a flat door placed on two supports, and are short on a cloth, a colorful bedsheet makes a decorative cover and is inexpensive and convenient to launder. Or search out an inexpensive, colorful washable "throw" or yard-wide felt in a striking color.

Not enough matching servings? Be chic: Mix-match what you have, in an alternated arrangement.

With the best planning—and the best of intentions—a party may need a little help from "props." That's where a theme comes in. If it's an unbirthday party, guests may all share in the honor; if it's Valentine's Day, even so-phisticates will warm up to a hearty theme in foods and decorations. Include an extrovert in every party list; his funny stories will help break the ice for all. Then en-courage the quiet ones to have their say. At any party, music can help set the mood and change the rhythm of the party according to your taste. If the room is crowded, however, and conversation flows, keep the music down to a quiet background effect. When you discover how much you enjoy your small parties, and how easy they become for you to do, you may never want to return to big bashes. But they have their advantages, too.

HOW TO RUN A BIG BASH AND ENJOY IT

At a big party, you may not be able to spend as much time talking with individual guests, but the interplay of the crowd can be even more stimulating.

What helps a big bash "take off"? Create a "some-thing's happening" effect as guests arrive—keyed to the interests of the guest of honor, or to a trip, or an occasion. Posters of old movies can set the stage for a celluloid fan's party; travel posters can brighten an "away from it all" party; a striking buffet setup may keynote your welcome; your bar can be set with glasses marked with each guest's name (easy with nail polish, easily removable afterward, and saves replacing glasses through the evening). Start conversation going with one guest, and then keep it going by introducing guests to each other. Encourage occasional shifts from group to group, and offer some new taste discoveries along with familiar favorites, to spark "Have you tried this?"

THE ART OF INVITING

Whether your invitation begins with an informal call— "Hi, I've been meaning to call to invite you . . ." or a written invitation, certain basic ground rules apply:

- Be definite about the time of arrival.
- Make sure the date is firmly established.
- Let your guests know the nature of the party and whether it is a special occasion.
- Indicate the time the party is likely to last . . . or that you want guests to linger as long as they like.

While it may seem a little more time-consuming at the start, written invitations actually take less time in the long run and serve as a party reminder to guests. Written invitations also are opportunities to enclose special travel directions or indicate the kind of occasion you plan.

If special dress would add to the fun of the party, or to your guests' enjoyment, indicate that "Dinner dress" will add to the anticipation of a meal into which you will put real effort. "Bring your bathing suit" or "Bring your sneakers" spell outdoor fun. And, of course, a costume party provides its own entertainment. Most important, a written invitation gives your guest a chance to think about the acceptance without being pinned down to a phone response—or evasion. Some people just would rather not dress up for a costume party! They can respond and ask for an invitation to your next party. And it's easier on you, too.

If you want to be sure to know who is coming to your party, write R.S.V.P. in the lower left-hand corner. Even people who have forgotten the complete French for "Respond if you please" recognize the initials. Add your phone number just below to simplify response.

A simpler system, newly popular—and practical— is to indicate *Regrets only* and your phone number.

HOW TO ENJOY YOUR OWN PARTY

The best test of a good party is whether you really enjoy it—from start to finish. You've done your best, worked out your plans, bought your supplies, set up the bar, and prepared the food—simple or simply superb. Now enjoy.

Enjoy your guests as you welcome them, make them feel at home, introduce them to each other—and to your home. Note when they want another drink, but don't rush one before a guest asks. Circulate . . . you will enjoy all your guests more and they will enjoy you more. Remember to replenish bar supplies, and keep a checklist of the menu handy in the kitchen, so you won't be in the position of the host who found the salad in the refrigerator after the party.

Enjoy your drinks, but pace sipping, rather than trying to keep up with *all* the guests. Space the food too, even as simply as by bringing out a bowl of carrot sticks, so that there are eating intervals between drinks. Bring on the music and light the candles or invite your friends to sing, at planned times—or shifting with the party mood.

The best part of a party is that you can't always predict what the best parts will be.

2

Design Your Home for Party Readiness!

Think of your living room—your home—as a reflection of your own lifestyle, your comfort and satisfaction. And for comfort and ease in welcoming your friends.

Whatever your choice in style and decor, you can copy it in your party plans. Casual style? That makes for relaxed parties at your home, fun with less work.

Little space? Your guests understand disposables, finger foods, and good drinks that are a salute to their good taste. Don't try formal service in small areas. Simplicity is a keynote, to make space stretch.

On the other hand, if you have ample space, flaunt it. With a dining room, relax at a sit-down meal.

FIRST IMPRESSION

Your welcome begins with an entry in keeping with your party theme, perhaps a pitcher of flowers or branches at the door, or a jack-o'-lantern for Halloween, or a brass bell tied to the doorknob for New Year's Eve that says "Welcome—I am expecting you," even before you meet at the door. Architects call this approach to the front of your home "elevation," and it can raise expectations for a good party.

FLOW—THE PARTY MOVES ON

Flow of guests, from arrival and doffing of overcoats, a welcoming first drink, to food arrangements and moving around in easy conversation . . . you need to structure this, a most important consideration in party layout. Whether guests gather in one room, an apartment, or a large home, keep three basic geometric shapes in mind for party flow: a triangle, a square, or a long, rectangular island. One of these steps will fit.

The Party Triangle in a large room, or in two rooms a three-sided pattern, is most likely the most efficient entertaining arrangement. If the door where your guests enter the room is one point of the triangle, set the bar at a second corner, and food at another opposite corner or other room, with some snack bowls in between.

THE PARTY TRIANGLE

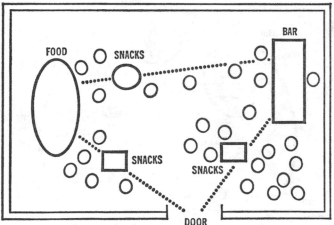

The Party Island provides a long thin line for guest service, around which guests can flow, and is ideal for a long, narrow room or for serving guests in a corridor outside another room. Set at the center of the room, a party island will make circulation possible all around the room all the time. Placed in a corridor, with auxiliary snack bowls inside other rooms, it can give guests reason to circulate and meet.

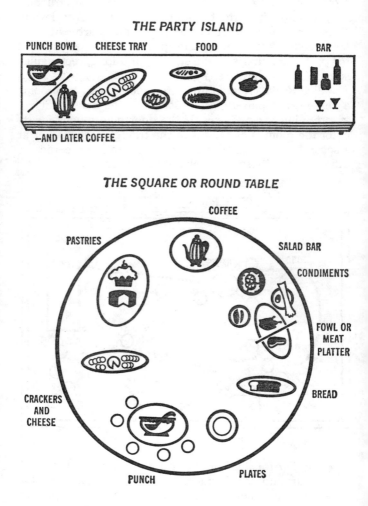

THE PARTY ISLAND

PUNCH BOWL   CHEESE TRAY   FOOD   BAR

—AND LATER COFFEE

THE SQUARE OR ROUND TABLE

COFFEE

PASTRIES   SALAD BAR

CONDIMENTS

FOWL OR
MEAT
PLATTER

BREAD

CRACKERS
AND
CHEESE

PUNCH   PLATES

The Square or Round Table in a corner of the living room or in the center of the dining room can serve for sit-down dining or buffet meals, with service bar in hall or kitchen. If the table is a buffet, a punch bowl will encourage self-service.

For a Smaller Party—you may be more concerned with conversational groupings of chairs. If your living room holds a sofa and a comfortable chair, add folding chairs or floor cushions in groupings arranged so that three or four people may talk with ease.

You can create new "island" groupings of chairs or cushions or add some small tables, plastic cubes, or even stacks of books to hold drinks, dishes, and ashtrays.

CONVERSATIONAL GROUPS

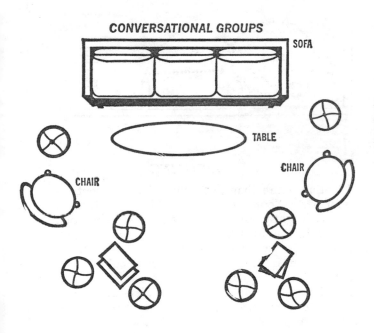

SOFA

TABLE

CHAIR

CHAIR

Traffic Routes—as you plan seating arrangements, keep traffic patterns in mind. If you plan to bring food and beverages in from a kitchen area, keep those "traffic lanes" uncluttered. Or set up a "sideboard" area, with a narrow table or board, to hold food as it is brought in. Keep paths open for "in" and "out" and for uncluttered movement around rooms.

For example:

TRAFFIC ROUTES

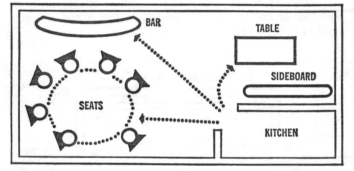

LIGHTING

Lighting, more than any other element, contributes to your party. Your entrance should be well lit, to welcome guests brightly, then lead them to a party room with direct lighting for the serving areas, and subdued, softer light in the rest of the room. Spotlights can illuminate individual arrangements, show off your hobbies or special acquisitions. Candlelight creates soft and romantic moods and flatters a dining table—and guests—gracefully.

And if guests linger and you want to signal the end of the party, putting on the bright lights will often do it.

There are a wide range of glasses for bar use. While fine glassware sets off great liquors to advantage if you plan a really large party, clear plastic on-the-rocks (six- to eight-ounce) glasses and highball glasses (12-ounce) may serve for most drinks. Use stemmed glasses for those who prefer cocktails or drinks without ice.

If you plan on serving hot drinks, mugs with handles are practical. Punch cups (or demitasse cups) are handy for self-serve drinks.

If you are short of storage space and want to stretch your glassware dollars, buy one attractive, roomy wine glass and use it for everything. Or add one heavy Old-Fashioned glass. Use the wine glass for many cocktails, cubed drinks, tall drinks, and aperitifs . . . as well as for wine, of course. Use the Old-Fashioned or on-the-rocks glass for cocktails, Scotch on the rocks, or other drinks.

3

Hospitality
Buying Guide

FROM "A" TO "B"—
ATTITUDES TO BUDGETS

If "A" stands for your Attitude in wanting a party, "B" stands for Budget—and how to entertain within your bounds in style. A good party is not necessarily expensive. Food can be as much fun when you serve Eggplant Parmesan Puffs as with Paté de Foie Gras; refreshing with a selective bar of favorite drinks, and as elegant in a simple set-ahead and serve-yourself buffet as with a fully staffed "sit-down" affair.

The attitude about what has "style" in party food and service has changed as much in recent years as the way we dress.

If you want to hire help or to use a caterer, your best bet is first to ask experienced friends for their recommendations. If no specifics are available, check your newspaper "lifestyle" editor for a list. Describe your needs and your party style, and specific names may be indicated. Or check your local directory, interview a number of caterers, and visit them, checking menus, styles of service, and budgets closest to your needs.

HOW MUCH HELP WILL YOU NEED?

Whether you hire a caterer or call on family or guests, it's realistic to have the following "hands" on tap for a big party . . . or realize you will likely have to draft some party helpers on the spot.

GUESTS	COCKTAILS	COCKTAILS BUFFET	SIT-DOWN DINNER
24	1 to serve 1 tending bar	2 to serve 1 in kitchen	3 to serve 1 in kitchen
48	2 to serve 1 tending bar	4 to serve 1 in kitchen	5 to serve 2 in kitchen
96	4 to serve 2 at bar	8 to serve 2 in kitchen	10 to serve 3 in kitchen

These are guidelines for a major party with help, but don't be intimidated if you want to swing it alone, letting your guests pitch in.

HOW DO YOU GO ABOUT MAKING SELECTIONS?

Your best buys in food and liquor come when you choose proper ingredients. Don't buy top sirloin to make Beef Bourguignon, for example—an end of steak or top round costs less and braises to tenderness. However, sometimes a filet is worth the price.

In buying liquor you want the very best for your guests, according to their tastes. For example, a Scotch-on-the-rocks connoisseur will appreciate The Glenlivet, a 12-year-old Scotch that is a compliment to good taste.

For those who want Scotch Sours or Rob Roys, The Famous Grouse offers distinctive Scotch flavor. Similarly, you can treat guests royally with Crown Royal if they enjoy smooth Canadian whisky on the rocks or as a mist or with water. Seagram's V.O. may be their choice in a Manhattan or distinguished mixed drinks. For more popular tastes, such as Seagram's 7 & 7-Up, or a ginger-ale highball, Seagram's 7 Crown is a great value.

To take advantage of the best values in liquors, you need to shop the brands you want in the most economical sizes for your party. In general, larger-size bottles offer savings in the cost per drink.

METRIC GUIDE

When you check liquor bottles on the shelf, note that sizes are now in the metric measure, virtually worldwide. Metric sizes are very close to U.S. equivalents—within a few ounces in most cases—but will be expressed in milliliters (ml.) or liters. A liter is 33.8 ounces, or just over our familiar quart, about a drink more per bottle.

METRIC BOTTLE CHART

METRICS	FLUID OUNCES	DRINKS PER BOTTLE
50 ml.	1.7	1
200 ml.	6.8	4–5
500 ml.	16.9	11
750 ml.	25.4	17
1 liter	33.8	22
1.75 liters	59.2	39–40

HOW MUCH LIQUOR WILL YOU NEED?

Plan to serve one to three drinks per hour per guest— depending on their size and tolerance. Know your guests —your experience may be your clue to their needs.

WHICH SIZE IS THE BEST TO BUY?

When you serve an assortment of drinks, you will be buying more bottles than you actually need. Choose large-sized bottles of the spirits you know your guests request most often, and smaller sizes of the "specialty" spirits or those some guests *might* ask for. If you buy economical sizes, you will be that much ahead for your next party! After the initial investment in starting a bar, keeping it in good supply is less costly and a satisfying party-readiness investment.

NUMBER OF DRINKS (at 1½ ounces per drink)	HOW MUCH YOU'LL NEED NUMBER OF BOTTLES	BOTTLE SIZE
1–17	1	750 ml. (or fifth)
1–21	1	liter (or quart)
22–39	1	1.75 liters
40–78	2	1.75 liters
79–117	3	1.75 liters
150	4	1.75 liters
300	8	1.75 liters
500	13	1.75 liters

HOW MANY KINDS OF LIQUOR DO YOU NEED?

If you *know* what your friends drink, you are safe to stock up mostly on the type they like—but be stocked for unexpected changes too.

Basic Six-bottle Budget Liquor Bar
American Whiskey—Seagram's 7 Crown
Bourbon—Benchmark Sour Mash Premium Bourbon
Canadian Whisky—Seagram's V.O.
Gin—Seagram's Extra Dry Gin
Scotch—The Famous Grouse
Vodka—Wolfschmidt

Choice Eight-bottle Liquor Bar
American Whiskey—Seagram's 7 Crown
Bourbon—Benchmark Sour Mash Premium Bourbon
Canadian Whisky—Seagram's V.O.
Gin—Seagram's Extra Dry Gin
Rum—Myers's Rum

Scotch—The Glenlivet
Tequila—Olmeca
Vodka—Wolfschmidt

Full Twelve-bottle Liquor Bar
American Whiskey—Seagram's 7 Crown
Bourbon—Benchmark Sour Mash Premium Bourbon
Canadian Whisky—Crown Royal, Seagram's V.O.
Gin—Seagram's Extra Dry Gin
Liqueurs and Cordials—your favorite Leroux
Rum—Myers's Rum
Scotch—The Glenlivet, The Famous Grouse
Tequila—Olmeca
Vodka—Wolfschmidt

SOME GOOD MIXERS

Think about your "mixers" for drinks as well as for people in planning your party. A completely new "mystery" drink such as the Wimbledon Whistle or the Squall can add fun to refreshment as guests guess the ingredients.

Icy water is the thriftiest mix! If the water in your area is cloudy, pour some decanters in advance, and let them stand in the refrigerator to clarify. For any party, you will need club soda for highballs—or special salt-free seltzer or mineral water for diet-conscious guests. Ginger ale may be the mixer for your group—or ginger beer can provide a zesty variant. Tonic, lemon-lime soda, and colas, with diet versions for some guests, are standards.

Look into fruit juices and Party Tyme instant freeze-dried cocktail mixes for quickly made drinks with plus flavor—and plus values.

ACCESSORIES TO ENTERTAINING

You will find a complete list of bar setups and accessories in Chapter 6. But you can plan a party even if you *don't* have a complete bar setup and want to save money. Let's take a look at what you are likely to need:

• *Ice:* The best ice is clear and sparkling, and purchased ice cubes are a good investment. Consider that a melted ice cube makes two ounces of water and costs under a penny for the two ounces. That's less than the cost of bottled mixers—and not much more than you pay if you freeze your own. If you are planning a party and really want to stretch pennies as well as dollars, freeze some cubes of your own, and store them in plastic bags.

To make clear cubes, boil the water first and let it cool before freezing (see Chapter 6). If you plan on serving punch, freeze some ice blocks, in molds or even washed milk cartons. Large blocks last longer and dilute the punch less. Freeze strips or slices of orange or lemon in the ice (see directions in Chapter 13) and the flavor will permeate the ice and your drinks—inexpensively.

• *Ice Buckets:* If you don't have an insulated ice bucket, set a mixing bowl into a larger bowl or plastic container, with about the same diameter at the top. A pocket of air is your insulator. After it is filled with cubes, cover the top of the bowl, and cubes will keep.

• *Bottle Opener:* There's no getting around this one —and no need to. Some stores supply openers; in any case, they cost little . . . and it's worth having party spares.

• *Corkscrew:* If you plan to serve wine, this is indispensable for cork-top bottles. You can, of course, choose wine bottled in decanters to solve this.

• *Jigger:* A marked measure, 1½ ounces.

• *Long-handled Mixing Spoon:* A pair of wooden chopsticks swirl well.

• *Cocktail Shaker with Top:* Shake up your drinks in any quart screw-top jar or insulated container with tight seal.

• *Lemon-lime Squeezer:* A fork stuck into the fruit will release the juice you need for a drink, with good control.

• *Stainless-Steel Knife:* Also multipurpose; a good one is worth buying.

• *Serving Tray:* If you run short, put decorative doilies or a towel on any flat board, or use the inverted lid of a sturdy carton or basket.

• *Coasters:* If you need more, use cocktail napkins under glasses.

SERVING GREAT FOOD—FOR LESS MONEY

Anyone could plan a great party with a large enough budget to call a good caterer and pick the top of the menu for the party. It's more satisfying to plan your own party and to end up with a more interesting menu just because you are watching your budget.

Here are ten points that can help you buy smartly for a party:

1. Don't be cautious. Be adventuresome! Try a new dish.

2. Study food prices before you plan your menu. Read the food ads and plan some items around the specials. If you have a recipe for a particular cut of meat or fruit or vegetable, and those particular ingredients are very expensive right now—substitute! For instance, if your marvelous veal scallopini is very expensive, make it with slices of turkey white meat or even with eggplant!

3. Sometimes a larger cut of meat for a party can be had for less than the per-pound steak cost. For instance, if you should see a luxury cut such as filet mignon at a fairly good price per pound, ask your butcher for the whole-cut price. It should be less per pound, and make an elegant dish affordable for you. Then you have the choice of cooking it whole, or cutting it into slices for filet mignon for an elegant feast.

4. Another technique worth using: Go to the market with a list of the number of portions and types of foods needed rather than a specific menu in mind. For example, if you want a pint of cheese dip, you have the choice of buying a cheese base or a cheese dip mix—but if you want a pint of dip and find avocados on sale, a pint of

zesty guacamole quickly made of mashed avocado can be your answer.

5. Figure out the yield in *servings* of what you are going to buy—not the purchase price.

Choose fruits and vegetables according to yield, too. Use an expensive item so that your menu has the advantage of its appeal, without featuring so much that the cost goes up. For example, asparagus might be too expensive to serve as a vegetable, but a pound of thin spears, bottoms scraped and imbedded in an ice bowl with other vegetables, will help make a distinguished bowl of *crudites* at modest overall cost.

6. Make the most of the price per unit, especially when you are buying party supplies. Check the price of the package *and* the price of a consistent measure, weight, or count. These are now posted on store shelves.

7. Check the freshness date of perishables, especially if you are buying supplies a few days in advance. However, if you are buying bread for a stuffing, for example, or tomatoes to cook in a sauce, you don't need the most perfect and may be able to save in shopping.

8. Some of your guests will be weight-conscious. Where foods include calorie statements on the labels, keep these in mind.

9. Take advantage of *all* the parts of what you buy. For instance, if you plan on a chicken casserole using three birds, save the livers for a gourmet spread.

10. Remember that sometimes less is more! A distinguished light menu will be memorable, satisfying, and make a party without regrets!

WISE ENERGY USE

If you can't stand the heat . . . don't get out of the kitchen! Just check these tips for saving energy when you cook. Experts calculate that only 40 per cent of the energy generated by your appliances actually goes into the food. The rest is lost. Some of that loss is avoidable.

Now with your party coming up, you'll want to save

needless costs. Your range, refrigerator, and freezer together are the third largest energy users in your home, so efficiency in the kitchen can mean big savings on utility bills. Some sensible steps in planning your cooking and serving will save energy—your own, as well as metered.

If it's a big bash, you probably have a lot of food to prepare, even if you're only serving hors d'oeuvre. If you use the oven, cook several foods in it at once. It's easier on you *and* on your utility bill. And use that microwave with consideration. It will heat your sauces or small quantities quickly and efficiently. But if you have thirty potatoes to bake, turn on the conventional oven. Good microwave bets for a party include stuffed mushrooms, and quiches baked in a glass tray. When you use the oven, resist the temptation to open the door every ten minutes to check on the progress of baking. Every opening loses about twenty-five degrees.

Using the right tool for the job also means fitting the pot to the burner. If the pot is much smaller than the electric coil, or if the gas flames overlap the sides of the pot, you're warming the kitchen as much as the food. Using the right pots on the right burner can mean a difference of as much as 30 percent in fuel use.

For a sit-down dinner party or for a buffet with cocktails, you'll likely have to keep foods warm for serving at intervals. If you've used your oven and turned it off, it will remain hot for quite a while. No need to keep it running. And if you're baking something, turn the oven off a little early. It will continue to cook with remaining residual heat.

Those beautiful electric chafing dishes and hot plates on your buffet table do a great job. But don't leave them running longer than necessary. They draw a lot of current. Well-insulated serving dishes help keep foods hot, especially if those tasty hors d'oeuvre disappear as quickly as they usually do.

You pay admission in extra energy when you open the refrigerator door. Decide what you need first, remove several items at once, and quickly close the door. Party time is cold-beverage time, and that means an especially big strain on the refrigerator. Better to fill some coolers with ice—it's cheap—than to reach into the refrigerator every time you need a chilled bottle.

Energy-saving cooking habits for parties magnify the usual preparation savings, because you are cooking and chilling foods in larger quantities. You can save 50 per cent in total energy use in cooking a meal, and energy-saving steps pay off in party savings.

*Whether it's a spicy dip,
a bouquet of nibbles,
flavorful kebabs or elegant
roulade...hors d'oeuvre
help spell your welcome*

Come on Over

Complete Home
Bartender's Guide

PART 2

Complete Home Bartender's Guide

All you want to know about distilled spirits and cordials

Bartender at home

Drink mixology...A to Z guide to 217 Bar Drinks Famous, Classic, and Contemporary

4

Your Guide to Distilled Spirits

Your favorite liquor is a product of nature that had its origins centuries ago. Science has since added technical controls for uniformity and flavor, but the basic process is the same as in 500 B.C. Later, in the twelfth century, alchemists searching for the elixir, the "water of life," distilled a remarkable liquid they called al-kohl. It may not have been the key to eternal youth for which they were seeking, but they were quick to recognize that it had special powers. In separating liquids from solids, they also learned to separate one liquid from another. Because alcohol boils and turns to vapor at a lower temperature than water, it came through distillation as a separate liquid.

Because this special "water" seemed to add something to life, the Gallic translation or *uisgebeatha* has become familiar here, in the form we call *whisky* if it is a Scottish or Canadian import. American-made whiskeys have the added "e."

Alcohol itself was known to man from time immemorial, since fermentation occurs naturally. Prehistoric man may have tasted the world's first "wine" when grapes fermented and the clear liquid was enjoyed.

DISTILLATION BECOMES A SCIENCE

Although alcohol develops naturally, distillation that separates and purifies is now a science. At Seagram the most advanced distillation processes are used to create and then keep consistent the unique flavors of our whiskies that are imported, as well as whiskeys made in the United States.

This process of distillation might be compared to the natural stages of bread-making. There are three stages in this process:

1. We begin with grains which go through *malting*, sprouting some of the grain to convert its starches to sugars. These are mashed. In the case of rum, sugar is the starting carbohydrate.

2. The resulting liquid is fermented with yeast. As in making bread, the type and amount of yeast, the temperature in the fermenting vats, and the time of fermentation are all important in determining the final quality of the spirit.

3. Distillation, the third step in making spirits, separates the alcohol from the rest of the mash. As indicated earlier, this is possible because alcohol boils and vaporizes at a lower temperature (176°F.) than water (212°F.).

THE FLAVOR ELEMENT

Congeners are what give flavor, body, and aroma— the characteristics you know—to the spirits. There's only about a teaspoonful of congeners in an average bottle of whiskey, but they are a very tasteful minority.

Some congeners come from the grain, some from the yeast, some even come from the water used in making the mash. Some of them make a beverage taste rich and smooth, others are best filtered out.

Distilling proof is different from the proof at which a liquor is drunk. The proof indicated on a bottle label stands for twice the alcohol content. If whiskeys were distilled at drinking proof (80 to 100 proof, or 40 percent to 50 percent alcohol), they would be very heavy with congeners—almost undrinkable. Seagram carefully determines the distilling proof to give the optimum flavor for the particular spirit and the drinking proof.

AGING

After distillation, most spirits, though not all, are drawn off into wood casks for aging. New whiskey from the still can be colorless and harsh, and it takes time, wood, and care to impart the characteristic amber color and mellow flavor.

Anyone who has ever looked at labels on a liquor store shelf knows that there are differences in aging from spirit to spirit and from brand to brand. Some spirits mature sooner than others. In general, the amount of aging necessary is related to the congeneric content; the heavier the body, the more aging is necessary. A light whiskey, for example, may need as little as four years of aging. Seagram's V.O. achieves unique smoothness and mellowness in six years, while The Glenlivet spends a full twelve years maturing in wood before it emerges as the definitive unblended whisky of Scotland. At the opposite extreme, Wolfschmidt Vodka—so carefully distilled that it is virtually free of congeners as it comes from the still, and therefore naturally smooth—requires no aging at all.

THE ART OF BLENDING

A fifth process, perhaps the most complex and demanding of all, is the fine art of blending, the marriage of a number of harmonious whiskeys—the whole to be greater than its parts.

Whiskey

Although we have been talking in general about all distilled spirits, the word "whiskey" keeps coming to the fore.

The federal government has a long, technical definition of whiskey that sets standards of identity. What it says, for our purposes, is that whiskey is distilled from grain, that it is distilled at low enough proof to give it a characteristic taste, and that it is aged.

Bourbon

No popular whiskey is more distinctly American than Benchmark Sour Mash Premium Bourbon, a product of the American heartland, made from at least 51 percent native American grain, corn. In fact, Bourbon has been recognized as a "distinctive product of the United States" by Congressional resolution, and no whiskey labeled "Bourbon" may be imported into the United States.

Benchmark's award-winning distillery is located in Louisville, Kentucky, in the middle of Bourbon country. But simply being steeped in Bourbon heritage doesn't make a great whiskey. Benchmark uses natural deep wells for cool, clear water and selects just the right yeasts and grains. From mashing through distillation and aging in oak barrels, the most particular care is taken to make a special American taste for the most particular palates.

The best-known Bourbon drinks include Bourbon Manhattan, cool Mint Julep, and hot Tom and Jerry (see Chapter 7). Cooking with Bourbon also flavors unique hamburgers and baked beans (see Recipe Index).

Other American Whiskeys

Many Americans prefer a blended flavor in tune with their tastes. This is as true of whiskey as of, for example, coffee, for which a variety of beans are blended to marry the aroma of one bean, the full body of another, and the mellowness of a third, to produce a truly exceptional brew. It takes a master blender's trained palate to create a balance of flavors in tune with today's tastes.

Blending to satisfy America's taste is what makes Seagram's 7 Crown the No. 1 whiskey in America today. From a "library of whiskeys," Seagram's master blenders select over fifty spirits that go into every bottle of Seagram's 7 Crown. Their challenge is to consistently produce a product that is superior whether enjoyed neat, on the rocks, or in mixed drinks.

Seagram's 7 Crown is America's favorite blended whiskey for Manhattans, and for the "7&7," 7 and Ginger, and Whiskey Sours (see Chapter 7).

Canadian Whisky

By law, any Canadian whisky sold in the United States must be at least two years old. And there is another law, governing all whiskies, that those under four years old must say so on the label. Seagram's V.O. is six years old. Since excellence is a function of how much is expended above and beyond the minimum, it's wise to look for the most respected names when you want the best, names like Crown Royal and Seagram's V.O.

Seagram's V.O. is a six-year-old blend of over one hundred aged whiskies, each distinctive, made in our distilleries in many parts of Canada to draw on the best of that nation's broad resources. Best-known drinks include V.O. Old-Fashioned, V.O. Highball, V.O. and Water and the Canadian Sour (see Chapter 7).

Fit for a King

Another fine tradition in whisky-making was begun in 1939. For the first time in history, a reigning British monarch was to visit Canadian soil. The reception had to be as extraordinary as the event.

As a fitting tribute to King George VI, the House of Seagram created an opulent whisky as a gift fit for a king. Blended from Seagram's finest whiskies, the liquor was put into an elegant crown-shaped bottle and a plush purple bag. Only fifty cases were prepared on that royal occasion, but the reaction was so enthusiastic that Crown Royal became a permanent member of the House of Seagram. Serve Crown Royal neat, like a brandy, or on-the-rocks, or with water or soda (see Chapter 7).

Scotch

Though its ancient lineage makes Scotch the classic whisky, its famous peat-fire and barley-malt taste place it in a class by itself among the spirits of the world. Scotch begins its life as barley which, after the harvest, is soaked and spread out on malting floors to sprout. This whole process takes about two weeks.

The next step is the one responsible for Scotch's characteristic smoky flavor. To stop the growth of the sprouting barley, the malt is taken to drying kilns, where it is spread out on screens over peat fires. As the heat dries the grain, the smoke permeates it and imparts aroma. Even the quality of the peat itself is a source of pride to Highland whisky-makers. Many an old-timer insists he can tell the source of the peat from the whisky taste.

From there on, the process is more familiar: mashing, fermentation, distillation, aging. But even here there are special differences that are part of the traditions of quality that Scotsmen hold with pride.

Each still has a glass box called a "spirits safe" to detect the presence of undesirable products and congeners in the distillate. The "spirits safe" enables the stillmaster to let the condensed liquid flow into the whisky receiver or to divert it back to the pot to be reseparated. The stillmaster is in control, and his skill affects the quality of the finished product.

After distilling, the new whisky is turned into casks, often used sherry casks, for aging. By law it must rest for at least three years. Most malt whiskies are more than five years old.

Unblended Scotch whiskies, such as The Glenlivet, also known as single malts, were until recently scarcely known outside their homeland, where each little distillery had its own loyal devotees. Except for an occasional bottle lovingly carried home from Scotland by a visitor who had fallen under the spell of these incredibly smooth potables, very little was seen on these shores. These single malts are critical to the "blends" of Scotch whiskies sold around the world.

THE GLENLIVET CROSSES THE SEA

Fortunately for Americans, and to the unparalleled delight of Scotch drinkers here, The Glenlivet, twelve years old, supreme among Scotch malts, was brought across the ocean. The most highly respected in Scotland, it is recognized as the most prestigious malt whisky in America, still made at the oldest licensed distillery in Scotland.

The most expensive ingredient in any whisky is time. The Glenlivet invests a full twelve years in its cherished potion. Drunk neat or with just a splash of water ("Don't drown the whisky," says the Scotsman), The Glenlivet reveals an incomparable depth of character that only this costly aging can produce.

The Glenlivet is best enjoyed neat, as a mist, with soda, with water or on-the-rocks.

SCOTCH BLENDS

We have been talking about single-malt Scotch all this time, but of course that is only part of the story. The secret of most of the other Scotches that the world enjoys is in the blending. Until about 1850, all Scotch whiskies were unblended whiskies. But about that time, ingenious whisky-makers, trying to arrive at new, lighter tastes, began blending the products of many widely separated distilleries. One outstanding result is The Famous Grouse.

Discover new enjoyment in a Rob Roy—a Manhattan made with Scotch—stirred up with The Famous Grouse. Or try Rusty Famous Grouse after dinner (see Chapter 7). And the smooth flavor of The Famous Grouse sets off Black Bean Soup to perfection (see index).

Gin

Many a man swears by the therapeutic qualities of his evening martini, the gin drink par excellence and aristocrat of cocktails. Small wonder, since gin was first distilled according to most accounts as a medicine, back in the days when herbal remedies were the rule. But because of the potion's palatability, it soon became popular in Europe as a beverage.

Gin has become drier and lighter in the past two centuries. It is flavored with juniper berries and distinctive botanicals and requires a very pure grade of alcohol.

The government prohibits any age claims on gin labels, but in fact Seagram's premium gin is aged in oak barrels to allow full flavor development. This is but one more reason why Seagram's Extra Dry is not only the "Perfect Martini Gin" (the ultimate test of quality gin), but also "perfect in all ways." While Seagram's is famous as the "Perfect Martini Gin" it also stands up well to tonic, makes a great Tom Collins, Red Baron, and Wimbledon Whistle. See Chapter 7.

Vodka

If we left the flavoring out of gin, we'd have something very like vodka. Grain neutral spirits, as we know, are distilled at a high proof, above 190° F., to eliminate as many congeners as possible. This almost, but not quite, qualifies a spirit to be vodka.

Government definition of this popular potion stipulates that it be distilled and processed "to be without distinctive character, aroma, or taste." If this is true, if vodka has no distinctive taste, then all vodkas are alike. Right? Wrong!

The challenge that each distiller must face is how to remove as many impurities as possible to produce a clean, smooth, pure beverage. Each maker faces the challenge in his own way, with varying degrees of success, but there are two basic methods for purifying vodka.

The first, and the standard method, is charcoal filtration. Every producer uses different equipment and favors charcoals made from different woods. The results are reflected in the many brands on the market.

The second method, pioneered by Wolfschmidt and one that even resulted in the U.S. government's changing its definition of vodka, is to distill the spirit so carefully that it emerges from the still as pure as man can make it.

Vodka's noble heritage began in the grain belt of Eastern Europe in the fourteenth century. (Grain, not potatoes! It is of course possible to distill vodka from potatoes, but many vodkas are and always have been made from grain.) Vodka was the favored drink of Imperial Russia. The Czars chose vodkas carefully, and Wolfschmidt was selected by the Romanof Household in 1860. Today it is the same premium vodka it was then. But we have learned to mix it and enjoy it in a range of drinks unheard of in the Czars' day! From Apple Eden to White Russian to Vodka Martini, vodka drinks span the seasons. See Chapter 7.

Rum

The first spirit drunk in the new American colonies was rum, a beverage associated with the seamen who brought it from the Caribbean Islands. Today, rum is rediscovering its early popularity as new generations of connoisseurs are drawn to a variety of exotic and refreshing tropical drinks, including Piña Colada, Mai Tai, and Planter's Punch.

Rum is a distilled spirit that is manufactured according to the same basic procedures as are whiskey, vodka, and gin. But in this case, the spirit's life begins not with grain but with cane—sugar cane.

In the manufacture of sugar, molasses is produced as a by-product when sugar crystals are extracted from the cane juice. This molasses is then fermented and distilled. The raw rum is aged in oak barrels for several years, after which it may be blended and bottled.

With the increasing popularity of tropical-style tall drinks, Americans are discovering the fuller, richer flavor of Myers's Rum, Platinum White and Golden Rich as well as the traditional Original Dark.

Daiquiris (including Strawberry), Planter's Punch, Hurricane, Mai Tai, Sunny Sour, Squall, Hot Toddy—you'll find a raft of rum drinks in Chapter 7.

Tequila

The national drink of Mexico has risen in popularity in the United States. Americans are discovering that this ancient beverage has its own sophisticated charms.

Tequila is distilled from the fermented juice of the maquey, or mezcal, a cactuslike plant that abounds in the Mexican deserts. This fermented juice, called pulque (prounced pull-kay,) is itself widely drunk by our neighbors to the south. The difference is that juice to be made into tequila is usually fermented more carefully.

Named for the town where the best of it is made,

tequila is distilled at a very low 104 proof, in order to retain the mash's natural flavors. Then, in the case of white tequila, it is drawn off into vats and bottled. Amber or golden tequila is aged for a time in wood, hence its color. Olmaco Tequila offers you a choice.

With the growing popularity of tequila in this country, the classic Margarita, compounded of tequila, triple sec, and lime, is becoming standard fare. Directions for Margarita, Bloody Bull, Sombrero, T 'n' T—and more—are in Chapter 7.

5

Cordials

Once the exclusive domain of after-dinner drinkers, who savored their cordials in small-stemmed glasses, or brandies in snifters, cordials or liqueurs now play new roles as cocktail mixers and cooking ingredients. With their range of flavors and sweet, smooth characteristics, they flavor and sweeten drinks in one easy step.

Distinctive flavor is the outstanding characteristic of cordials, which are composed of a distilled spirit, a sweetener, and essence of fruit or seed or bark or flower flavor. No wonder they work such mixing magic.

Cordials also flavor many dishes effectively. Try appetizer cheese straws flavored with kümmel, duckling flavored with sloe gin, a dash of crème de Noya in your peach pie, or crème de cacao in your cacao chocolate mousse . . . just for starters.

CORDIAL BEGINNINGS

Cordials begin as distilled spirits. In theory, any of the spirits discussed in Chapter 4 may be used, and in fact, an occasional liqueur is made on a rye, Scotch, or Bourbon base. In practice, though, most cordials are made from either brandy or neutral spirits.

Neutral spirits, as discussed in the previous chapter, are generally made from grain and distilled at a very high proof so as to be smooth, clear, and pure. One of the hallmarks of Leroux cordials is the purity of the base.

FLAVORED BRANDIES

Flavored brandy liqueurs, on the other hand, combine the depth and finesse of a fine brandy with a variety of enticing fruit, herb, and spice flavors.

Brandy is distilled and aged in much the same manner as fine whiskeys. But in this case, it is distilled not from a fermented grain mash, but from a mash of fermented grapes—in other words, wine. In fact, the word brandy comes to us from the Dutch *brandewijn,* meaning "burned wine." Strictly speaking, a brandy is any spirit, aged or unaged, distilled from fruit. But usually the word "brandy" alone refers to a grape distillate. Brandies made from other fruits are usually named after that fruit.

There's one other kind of spiritous beverage worth knowing: white fruit brandies. Though these clear spirits are generally classed with cordials or liqueurs (the two words mean the same thing), they are not cordials because they are not sweetened.

Unaged to retain their fresh-fruit aromas, these are distilled from a variety of fruits other than grapes. The most notable example of this type is Leroux Kirschwasser, a fresh, aromatic clear brandy made from cherries and cherry pits. Other brandies are made from plums, raspberries, and pears.

Now let's look, one by one, at the most popular cordials.

A GUIDE TO CORDIAL SPIRITS

Abisante—A subtle anise flavor in a pale green liquid. For a dazzling cocktail or aperitif, a delight to the eye as it is to the palate, let Abisante drip slowly over ice and watch its clear green change to a creamy, opalescent cloud. Or for a classic cocktail make a Sazerac (p. 173). It's a delightful seasoning for vegetables, fish. . . .

Amaretto—Imported from Italy, with the matchless

taste of almonds. Try it neat, to savor its full flavor. Make an Italian Soother (p. 94). A dash goes well over vegetables and many desserts.

Anesone—Similar to Anisette in flavor but slightly drier and stronger in alcoholic content. Its licorice flavor blends well with hot coffee or with Leroux Coffee Brandy.

Anisette—In white or red, the classic licorice-flavored liqueur, made from anise seeds.

Apple Flavored Brandy—The taste of the best apples with a fine brandy base. For a refreshing cold drink make a Jack Rose cocktail. Leroux Apple Flavored Brandy is a natural with light meats. Use it for basting a pork loin roast or flavoring veal cutlets.

Apricot Flavored Brandy—The mellow taste of apricots in a versatile and satisfying distillation. It is essential in an Apricot Sour (see Chapter 7).

Apricot Liqueur—Rich, sweet, and fruity. It adds new interest to custard sauces and fruit compotes.

Aquavit—A colorless, potent beverage originally from Scandinavia. It is unsweetened and takes its chief flavor from the caraway seed. Mixed with tomato juice and a squeeze of lime, it makes a Danish Mary. The Scandinavians drink it ice cold and straight.

Blackberry Flavored Brandy—Made from genuine, ripe blackberries. It's a popular liqueur neat or on the rocks, with soda, or in a Seven Blackberry Fizz (p. 78).

Blackberry Liqueur—Slightly sweeter than Blackberry Flavored Brandy.

Cherry Flavored Brandy—One of the all-time favorite fruit flavored brandies. For a marvelously natural fruit flavor, serve Leroux Cherry Flavored Brandy over crushed ice, with straws, or in a Seven Cherry Sour (p. 80).

Cherry Karise—The famous, imported Danish liqueur from sweet Dalmatian cherries. Served straight or on-the-rocks, it is an impressive after-dinner drink. Or trickle a little over vanilla ice cream.

Cherry Liqueur—Another cherry flavored cordial,

this one a bit sweeter and less tart. For an elegant dessert, pour one ounce Leroux Cherry Liqueur over ripe sweet cherries in a champagne glass and fill with champagne.

Chocolate Amaretto—Two of the most luscious flavors, chocolate and almond, in a single liqueur. For a delicious cocktail, add a splash to Myers's Rum and soda over ice. Spoon Leroux Chocolate Amaretto over desserts.

Claristine—A herb liqueur made from a secret formula discovered by the Clarisse nuns of Dinant, Belgium. Connoisseurs sip it straight, at room temperature, for a soothing after-dinner *digestif*. Makes an unusual cocktail or highball with brandy to make a C&B cocktail.

Coffee Flavored Brandy—Made from one of America's favorite beverage flavors. Leroux Coffee Flavored Brandy combines the richest Colombian coffees—with the finest brandies. It's delicious by itself or with cream, in hot coffee, or in a Black Russian.

Cognac à l'Orange—One of the most distinguished of orange flavored cordials. Imported from France, Leroux Cognac with orange is a blend of fine aged Cognac and thrice-distilled orange. Try substituting it for other orange liqueurs in your favorite cocktail, like the Margrita (see Chapter 7) or in creams, cheesecake, crepes, and other dishes.

Crème de Banana Liqueur—The taste of the Caribbean in a sweet liqueur. Because it is blended from the finest natural fruit flavors, with nothing artificial added, Leroux Crème de Banana Liqueur makes the perfect Banana Daiquiri (p. 67).

Crème de Cacao—The classic chocolate liqueur, brown or white. For Alexanders and a great partner with Myers's Rum and pineapple juice in a refreshing tall drink.

Crème de Cafe—A sweet, coffee-flavored spirit. Add an ounce of Leroux Crème de Cafe to a glass of cold milk for a soothing drink.

Crème de Cassis—A specialty of France, made from the juice of black currants. For a refreshing aperitif, add an ounce to a glass of chilled white wine to make a Kir cocktail or a Gin Kir cocktail (see Chapter 7).

Crème de Menthe—Mint flavor in a green or white sweet liqueur. Real mint leaves give Leroux a fresh taste that's never cloying. Classic in V.O. Stinger as well as the Hurricane Cocktail (see Chapter 7).

Crème de Noya—A ruby-hued cordial created from a blending of almond flavors. It gives an exotic, fruity taste and aroma to a Myers's Mai Tai. Shake a Pink Squirrel.

Curaçao—An orange liqueur made somewhat like Triple Sec, but with the addition of spices, port wine, and rum to give a distinctive slightly tart flavor. Countless uses in the kitchen and the bar. Select Leroux Blue Curaçao for a Blue Devil (see Chapter 7).

Fraise de Bois—Imported Austrian liqueur with the taste of wild strawberries. Straight, it makes a fragrant after-dinner cordial added to white wine, an aperitif.

Ginger Flavored Brandy—A hearty beverage of American origin, with the flavor of fresh ginger root. Anyone who likes ginger ale in his tall drinks will discover many new ways to mix Leroux Ginger Flavored Brandy.

Gold-O-Mint—The cool taste of Crème de Menthe, with a golden color.

Grenadine Liqueur—Pomegranate syrup with a low alcoholic content. Leroux Grenadine is an ingredient in mixed drinks and cocktails and tall drinks made with fruit juices. The Tequila Sunrise is best-known (Chapter 7).

Kirschwasser—Not a cordial, but a dry, white, unaged brandy distilled from cherries and cherry pits. In Europe, Kirschwasser is sipped straight, as an after-dinner drink, and is widely used for flavoring.

Kümmel—A clean, dry (unsweetened) spirit with the taste of caraway. It's good straight, in cocktails, or sprinkled over cabbage, cauliflower, or beets.

Maraschino—A clear, sweet liqueur made from small, black Marasca cherries; using some of the pits in distillation gives it an almondy flavor. Its smoothness makes it a perfect mixer. Use in mixed drinks.

Ouzo—A Greek-style spirit with the flavor of Anisette but with higher proof and low sugar content.

Peach Flavored Brandy—Made from fresh peaches and fine brandy. Sip over ice or make a Peach Sour: variation of Apricot Sour (see Chapter 7).

Peach Liqueur—Peach flavor with a pure neutral spirit base. For a tangy, fruity cocktail, shake 1½ ounces Leroux Peach Liqueur and ¾ ounce lemon juice with ice and strain. For an exciting dessert splash over berries.

Peppermint Schnapps—Similar to white crème de menthe, but drier and lighter. If you like a dry Stinger, substitute Leroux Peppermint Schnapps for crème de menthe.

Raspberry Liqueur—Flavored with, of course, raspberries. Polish-style Leroux Malinowy Raspberry Liqueur is noted for its delicate fruit flavor.

Rock and Rye—There are two different types, both made with rye whiskey and sugar: Rock and Rye with Fruits, made with a mixture of fruits including oranges, lemons, and cherries; and Irish Moss Rock and Rye, with pure sugar crystals in the bottle, for Old-Fashioneds.

Sambuca—Imported Italian liqueur with a licorice-like taste but more subtle than Anisette. Leroux Sambuca is enjoyed straight, in hot coffee, or with tonic and lime. Use it to flavor broiled or sautéed shrimp.

Sloe Gin—A gin-based fine cordial made with a tiny wild European plum called the sloeberry. Its most popular cocktail is the Sloe Gin Fizz.

Strawberry Liqueur—Sophisticated strawberry flavor. Adds the perfect touch to the Strawberry Daiquiri.

Triple Sec—The most popular of all orange-flavored liqueurs. Leroux Triple Sec is a colorless beverage made from the peels of Curaçao oranges. Indispensable in many cocktails, such as the Margarita and the Gin Sidecar (see Chapter 7) and in the preparation of Crepes Suzette.

6

Bartender Techniques at Home

First off, you need to stock a bar with liquors and with setups that include everything else you need to mix drinks, from mixers through ice and accessories for making drinks to hold them. Of all the steps to party preparation, a well-set bar at whatever scale ranks high in establishing your party-readiness. A well-thought-out bar plan makes party-giving easier for you.

Let's look at bar setups at three levels:

1. POSH BAR—a situation where you can afford the ideal in time and money. Your bar might be located in a small room with several easy chairs or in a portion of the living room. It is built into a wall behind a panel that swings open. A ledge pulls up for easy service when the door opens. Shelves hold your range of bottles and mixers; there is a small refrigerator to chill supplies, and possibly an ice-cube maker. A blender for whirring up frothy drinks is at hand and a full battery of bar accessories. This is inspiration for gracious entertaining.

2. UP-SCALE BAR—great quality, but not built in. This can be housed in or on an ample rolling cart, with shelf to hold additional supplies and accessories. It has the added convenience of mobility, ease of stocking in the kitchen, and then moving where you want to serve.

3. PARTY BAR SETUP—set this up for your party on a chest or a sturdy folding table covered with a cloth or on a tray, checking the bar accessory lists to be certain

CORKSCREWS

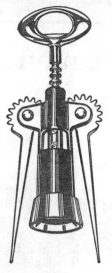

WING

SUCTION

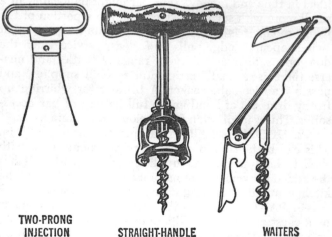

TWO-PRONG INJECTION

STRAIGHT-HANDLE

WAITERS

you have what you need on hand and borrowing accessories such as small knife and blender or beater from your kitchen.

Whichever setup you have, here are the guidelines you need to stir up drinks like a pro.

BAR EQUIPMENT CHECK LIST

1 jigger measure
1 small, pointed paring knife—the best you can find is a low-cost, worthy investment; use stainless steel for cutting lemons and limes.
1 lemon squeezer (will do for oranges and limes, too).
1 fine strainer.
1 long-handled bar spoon.
1 corkscrew—check types when you shop, to find which you use most comfortably:

- waiters
- wing
- straight-handle
- suction
- 2-prong injection.

bottle-cap opener.
ice crusher or ice shaver—manual or electric.
toothpicks—sturdy wood or plastic, to hold cherries, olives, other garnishes.
1–2 big mixing glasses or straight pitchers, with strainer that fits snugly and a pouring top, to stir cocktails.
1 cocktail shaker or a blender.
1 large shaker jar, about 2-quart capacity.
1 bar apron, at least when you are setting up.
bar towel
ice bucket and tongs

MORE ABOUT GLASSES
(See also Chapter 2)

Use larger glasses rather than smaller ones, but not to hold more per drink. Liquor aromas (as well as wines) breathe better in larger glasses, and you will avoid spills.

Stemmed glasses are practical for all cocktails and heavily iced drinks. They are easier to hold in your hand without frostbite; the heat of the hand doesn't take the chill from the drink. That's why we recommend a sturdy stemmed goblet for most drinks. For traditionalists who prefer drinks in a heavy glass, use a double Old-Fashioned for most uses. For special drinks, such as a tall Hurricane, you might want an extra-tall glass; hot drinks are more comfortable to hold in mugs.

How Many Glasses Should You Stock?

The restaurant rule of thumb for glassware is to compute the number (maximum) of guests you will serve at any one time, and multiply it by 2½ to allow for refills, breakage, and unexpected drop-ins. This means that if you expect eight guests you would be safest to have about twenty glasses of the types they are likely to use.

Keep Them Sparkling

Freshly washed glasses will dry sparkling if you place them face down on a folded towel. Or dry with one towel, polish with a second. Glasses should be washed as soon as possible. Don't let them sit around until the next morning. If you don't feel like doing them the night of the party, fill a sink with clean hot water and detergent, a splash of vinegar and let them soak overnight. Never stack glasses together. If you do and they stick and will not separate, place the bottom glass in warm-hot water and fill the top glass with cold water. The difference in expansion will free up the glasses.

THE BASIC BAR INVENTORY

The most popular-sized bottles for home bars are the 750-milliliter or the liter, which pour about 17 drinks and 22 drinks, respectively. If you use larger quantities of one type, buy that variety in the 1.75-liter party size.

To "inventory" your stock quickly, do as the bartenders do—divide your bottle into 10s by eye, and if you see you have 3/10s left in a 750-milliliter bottle, you know that you have about 5 drinks left in the bottle.

The basic bar should include the following:

Whiskey and Whisky

> Blended Whiskey—Seagram's 7 Crown
> Bourbon—Benchmark Sour Mash Premium Bourbon
> Canadian Whiskies—Seagram's V.O., Crown Royal
> Scotch Whisky and Scotch Whisky Blend—The Glenlivet, The Famous Grouse (one or more each)

Gin—Seagram's Extra Dry Gin
Rum—Myers's Rum
Tequila—Olmeca
Vodka—Wolfschmidt Vodka
Aperitifs, Mixers:
> Leroux Liqueurs (as sippers and as mixers)

Wines:
> Basic White—Paul Masson Chablis
> Basic Red—Paul Masson Burgundy

Vermouths:
> Paul Masson Sweet Vermouth
> Paul Masson Double Dry Vermouth

MIXERS, TRIMMINGS AND GARNISHES

To go along with the basic bar, you need nonalcoholic offerings, mixers, and accompaniments for combining drinks and also to provide nonalcoholic drinks for younger guests or drinkers sitting one out. Use this for your bar check list:

club soda
ginger ale
tonic water
7-Up
cola
bitters
Tabasco sauce
Worcestershire sauce
maraschino cherries
grenadine
tomato juice
grapefruit juice
pineapple juice
spring water

orange juice
apple juice
cranberry juice
½ pint light or heavy cream
superfine bar sugar
lemons/limes
large navel orange, sliced
sweetened lime juice
cream of coconut (can)
assorted fruits, fresh such
    as bananas, or frozen in
    heavy syrups such as
    strawberries (for frozen
    daiquiris)

THE BARTENDER'S GUIDE

1. Always measure, using a jigger. A too-strong drink is off balance and throws your guests off, too.

2. *Stir* drinks that should be sparkling clear, such as martinis or Manhattans.

3. *Shake* drinks for a frothy top, such as sours.

4. *Blend or beat* drinks that should be foamy throughout, such as Piña Colada or many fruit drinks— or a sour or Bloody Mary if you want it foamy throughout. Ice becomes aerated if you whirl it with the drink in a blender, or shake it hard enough.

5. Serve cold drinks frosty cold. Chill the glasses if at all feasible.

6. Serve hot drinks very hot, in handled mugs. To avoid cracking, place a silver spoon in the glass before pouring a hot beverage.

7. Ice goes into the glass or mixer first.

8. Liquor gets poured over ice for clear cocktails; modifying ingredients are then added.

9. When sugar or fruit juices are added, these go into the glass first, then liquor is added.

10. Your drinks can't be better than the liquor you use. That is why Seagram balances blends so carefully, ages liquors in their own barrels, follows traditional procedures with constant quality control in making the liquors suggested for your bar.

Frosted Glasses or Mugs

Place glasses or mugs in the refrigerator or bury in shaved ice until the glass frosts over.

To Serve Vodka in Clear Ice Block

Remove top and wash 46-ounce juice can or ½-gallon milk container. Set bottle in center of container, fill with water. Place straight up in freezer, and freeze solid. To release ice-jacketed bottle, let stand about 15 minutes in a warm place, then slip out of container. After it is frozen, the iced bottle can be returned to freezer between uses, wrapped in a plastic bag.

To Rim Glasses With Sugar or Salt

Place ¼-inch lemon or lime juice in a saucer. Dip rim of glass in this, then dip into superfine sugar or coarse salt, per recipe.

To Prepare Simple Syrup

Syrup is simple to prepare and it keeps indefinitely at the bar. To make simple bar syrup: dissolve 1 pound of granulated sugar—about 2¼ cups—in one cup of boiling water. Gradually add another cup of water, stirring until clear. Makes 1 pint. Cool and pour into clean bottle.

To Cut and Use Twists

Use a vegetable scraper, and you will be able to shave thin twists from lemon without picking up any of the bitter inner rind. Or hold your knife almost parallel with the fruit, and cut thin strips. To use, rub the outer skin of the peel around the rim of the glass to coat it with the natural, flavorful oil. Then twist the peel over the glass to add more to the oil. Finally, drop the twist in.

BE PREPARED

Before a large party, preseason a pitcher of tomato juice for Bloody Marys, or prepare a pitcher of Daiquiri mixture or Piña Colada mixture. Add liquor and shake or blend just before serving.

Sweet and Sour Mix, for Sours or Other Drinks

Use a Party Tyme freeze-dried cocktail mix, or frozen concentrate for lemonade, to flavor your drinks. Frozen concentrate for limeade works fine, too. Or make your own with fresh fruit and sugar.

BAR MEASURES AND EQUIVALENTS

1 jigger, or 1 bar glass—1½ ounces or 45 milliliters
1 teaspoon—⅙ ounce or 5 milliliters
1 tablespoon—½ ounce or 15 milliliters
1 cup—8 ounces
1 coffee cup—6 ounces
1 dash—4 drops
1 pony—1 ounce

7

Drink Mixology

From Acapulco to Zombie, 217 drinks in this chapter can qualify you as the home bartender *extraordinaire*.

These drinks include well-known classics in each liquor category, and others to add fun and variety—including directions for making your own specialty.

Your favorite liquor? Here is your guide to the many bar drinks in each liquor category. The number next to each drink is your key to the 217 recipes that follow.

CANADIAN WHISKY

SEAGRAM'S V.O.—The nation's leading premium Canadian whisky, preferred throughout the world.

CROWN ROYAL—The legendary whisky to a King's taste, made with the rarest whiskies of Canada.

CROWN ROYAL MIST	59	EARTHQUAKE	69
CROWN ROYAL NEAT	60	INK STREET	101
CROWN ROYAL AND SODA	61	SINGAPORE COLLINS	167
CROWN ROYAL, WATER	62	WASHINGTON NORTH	203

AMERICAN WHISKEY

SEAGRAM'S 7 CROWN—Quality drinks begin with America's favorite whiskey, on-the-rocks or mixed.

APRICOT SOUR	3	PERFECT MANHATTAN	111
BLINKER	13	MAPLE 7 SOUR	112
BOLIVAR COCKTAIL	19	NEW YORKER	120
CAFE 7	46	OLD-FASHIONED	122
CHERRY SOUR	53	7 & GINGER OR COLA	164
COWBOY	58	7 & 7	165
FIRECRACKER	73	SKY CLUB	168
HORSE'S NECK	95	TOM AND JERRY	184
LONG ISLAND TEA	107	VALENCIA	186
MANHATTAN	109	WHISKEY SOUR	205
DRY MANHATTAN	110	WHITE SHADOW	210

SCOTCH

THE GLENLIVET—The twelve-year-old Father of all Scotch sets the world's highest standard.

SCOTCH MIST	152	SCOTCH ON THE ROCKS	155
SCOTCH NEAT	153	SCOTCH AND WATER	160

THE FAMOUS GROUSE—A distinctive favorite of Scotland, blended for flavor, aged for smoothness.

BAIRN	5	SCOTCH SMASH	156
BARBARY COAST	7	SCOTCH AND SODA	157
ROB ROY	137	SCOTCH SOUR	158
DRY ROB ROY	138	SCOTCH SWIZZLE	159
PERFECT ROB ROY	139	STONE FENCE	171
RUSTY FAMOUS GROUSE	147	THISTLE	181
SCOTCH BUCK	151	WHITE SCOTCH	209
SCOTCH OLD-FASHIONED	154		

BOURBON

BENCHMARK SOUR MASH PREMIUM BOURBON
—It's in a class by itself . . . pour it with arrogance.

ADMIRAL COCKTAIL	2	BOURBON SWIZZLE	36
BENCH AND BULL	9	BOURBON TEA	38
BENCHMARK MOCHA	10	BOURBON AND TEA	37
BOURBON AND BITTERS	23	BOURBON TODDY	39
BOURBON AND BRANCH	24	BOURBON WARD EIGHT	40
BOURBON AND COFFEE	25	BOURBON AND WATER	41
BOURBON COLLINS	26	CLIQUET	56
BOURBON DAISY	27	DIXIE WHISKEY	68
BOURBON FIZZ	28	EGGNOG	70
BOURBON HIGHBALL	29	GOLDEN GLOW	92
BOURBON LANCER	30	HOT APPLE KNOCKER	96
BOURBON MANHATTAN	31	MINT JULEP	117
BOURBON MIST	32	SAZERAC	150
BOURBON RICKEY	33	TOM AND JERRY	184
BOURBON SMASH	34	YELLOWBIRD	214
BOURBON SOUR	35	ZERO MINT JULEP	215

RUM

MYERS'S RUM—The full, rich rum taste. More flavor for your favorite rum drinks.

ACAPULCO	1	FOX TROT	76
BANANA DAIQUIRI	6	GOLDEN GLOW	92
BARBARY COAST	7	GROG	94
BLACK STRIPE	12	HOT APPLE KNOCKER	96
BOLO	20	HOT BUTTERED RUM	97
BOSTON TEA HARDY	22	HOT TODDY	98
BROWN DERBY	44	HURRICANE PUNCH	100
CARIBBEAN COOLER	52	JOLLY ROGER	103
CHRISTOPHE	55	LONG ISLAND TEA	107
CLIQUET	56	MAI TAI	108
DAIQUIRI	63	PANAMA	125
DAIQUIRI DELUXE	64	PEACH DAIQUIRI	127
DAIQUIRI — FROZEN	65	PIÑA COLADA	128
FLORIDA PUNCH	74	PINEAPPLE DAIQUIRI	129
FLORIDITA SPECIAL	75	PLANTER'S PUNCH	131

GIN

SEAGRAM'S EXTRA DRY GIN—The Perfect Martini Gin, just as perfect in other mixed drinks.

VODKA

WOLFSCHMIDT VODKA—Made by special appointment to His Majesty the Czar.

Apple Eden	4	Russian Bear	146
Black Russian	11	Salty Dog	148
Bloody Caesar	14	Screwdriver	161
Bloody Mary	16	Vodka Collins	187
Blushing Wolf	18	Vodka Fizz	188
Bull Shot	45	Vodka Flip	189
Cape Codder	51	Vodka Gibson	190
Clamdigger	54	Vodka Gimlet	191
Cobbler	57	Vodka Martini	192
Licorice Slush	105	Vodka Twist	193
Long Island Tea	107	Volga Boatman	194
Moscow Mule	118	Wallbanger	201
Ninotchka	121	Watermelon Cooler	204
Purple Passion	133	White Russian	208
Raspberry Cooler	135	Wolf and Tonic	212

TEQUILA

OLMECA TEQUILA—The truly memorable tequila, Mexico's sunny best.

Acapulco	1	Tequila Rickey	176
Bloody Maria	15	Tequila Sour	177
El Diablo	71	Tequila Sunrise	178
Margarita	113	Tequila Sunstroke	179
Matador	116	Tequila and Tea	180
Sangrita	149	T 'n' T	182
Sombrero Mexicali	169	Xylophone	213

1. ACAPULCO

Myers's Rum	¾ ounce
Olmeca Tequila	¾ ounce
pineapple juice	1½ ounces
grapefruit juice	2 teaspoons

Shake with ice. Strain into a chilled cocktail glass.

2. ADMIRAL COCKTAIL

Benchmark Sour Mash Premium Bourbon	1 ounce
dry vermouth	1½ ounces
lemon juice	½ ounce

Shake with ice. Strain into a chilled cocktail glass. Garnish with lemon twist.

3. APRICOT SOUR

Seagram's 7 Crown	¾ ounce
Leroux Apricot Flavored Brandy	¾ ounce
lemon juice	½ ounce
sugar	½ teaspoon

Shake with ice. Strain into a chilled sour glass. Garnish with a lemon slice and a Maraschino cherry.

4. APPLE EDEN

Wolfschmidt Vodka	1½ ounces
apple juice	3 ounces

Pour over ice cubes in an Old-Fashioned glass. Stir. Garnish with an orange twist.

5. BAIRN

The Famous Grouse Scotch	*1 ounce*
Leroux Triple Sec	*½ ounce*
orange bitters	*1 dash*

Shake with ice. Strain over cubes in Old-Fashioned glass.

6. BANANA DAIQUIRI

Myers's Rum	*1½ ounces*
lemon or lime juice	*½ ounce*
banana, sliced	*¼*
sugar	*1 teaspoon*
crushed ice	*½ cup*

Whirl all in a blender until smooth. Pour into a chilled champagne glass.

7. BARBARY COAST

The Famous Grouse Scotch	*½ ounce*
Seagram's Extra Dry Gin	*½ ounce*
Myers's Rum	*½ ounce*
Leroux White Crème de Cacao	*½ ounce*
cream	*½ ounce*

Shake with ice. Strain over cubes in Old-Fashioned glass.

8. BARNUM

Seagram's Extra Dry Gin	*1 ounce*
Leroux Apricot Flavored Brandy	*½ ounce*
bitters	*2 dashes*
lemon juice	*1 dash*

Shake with ice. Strain over cubes in Old-Fashioned glass.

9. BENCH AND BULL

Benchmark Sour Mash Premium Bourbon   1½ ounces
beef bouillon   3 ounces

Shake with ice. Strain over ice cubes into an Old-Fashioned glass. Garnish with cucumber slices.

10. BENCHMARK MOCHA

Benchmark Sour Mash Premium Bourbon   1½ ounces
strong hot coffee   3 ounces
sweetened hot chocolate   3 ounces

Combine Bourbon, coffee, and chocolate in a mug. Stir.

11. BLACK RUSSIAN

Wolfschmidt Vodka   1 ounce
Leroux Crème de Café   ½ ounce

Shake with ice. Strain over ice cubes in an Old-Fashioned glass. Garnish with an orange twist.

12. BLACK STRIPE

Myers's Rum   1½ ounces
molasses   ½ teaspoon
boiling water

Mix rum and molasses in a cup or small mug. Fill with boiling water. Stir. Garnish with a lemon twist.

13. BLINKER

Seagram's 7 Crown	1½ ounces
grapefruit juice	3 ounces
Leroux Grenadine	½ ounce

Shake with ice. Strain over ice cubes in an Old-Fashioned glass.

14. BLOODY CAESAR

Wolfschmidt Vodka	1½ ounces
Tabasco sauce	Dash
Clamato (clam-tomato cocktail)	

Pour vodka over ice in a goblet. Add Tabasco. Fill with Clamato drink. Stir. Garnish with a lime wedge.

15. BLOODY MARIA

Olmeca Tequila	1½ ounces
lime juice	½ ounce
Tabasco sauce	Dash
celery salt	Dash
tomato juice	

Pour tequila, lime juice, Tabasco, and celery salt over ice cubes in a highball glass. Fill with tomato juice. Stir. Garnish with a lime slice.

16. BLOODY MARY

Wolfschmidt Vodka	1½ ounces
lemon juice	½ ounce
Worcestershire sauce	1 dash
Tabasco sauce	1 dash
celery salt	1 dash
tomato juice	

Pour vodka, lemon juice, and seasonings over ice cubes in a highball glass. Fill with tomato juice. Stir. Garnish with a lime wedge or a celery stalk.

17. BLUE DEVIL

Seagram's Extra Dry Gin	1½ ounces
Leroux Blue Curaçao	½ ounce
lemon juice	½ ounce

Shake with ice. Strain into a chilled cocktail glass. Garnish with a lemon slice.

18. BLUSHING WOLF

Wolfschmidt Vodka	1½ ounces
Leroux Grenadine	1 dash
grapefruit juice	

Pour vodka and grenadine over ice cubes in a highball glass. Fill with grapefruit juice. Stir.

19. BOLIVAR COCKTAIL

Seagram's 7 Crown	1½ ounces
Leroay Abisante	4 dashes
lemon juice	1 ounce
sugar	1 teaspoon

Shake with ice. Strain into a sour glass. Garnish with a slice of orange.

20. BOLO

Myers's Rum	1½ ounces
lemon juice	½ ounce
orange juice	½ ounce
sugar	½ teaspoon

Shake with ice. Strain into a chilled cocktail glass. Garnish with a lemon slice.

21. BOOMERANG

Seagram's Extra Dry Gin	1½ ounces
Paul Masson Double Dry Vermouth	½ ounce
lime juice	½ ounce

Shake with ice. Strain into a chilled cocktail glass. Garnish with a lime slice.

22. BOSTON TEA HARDY

Myers's Rum	1½ ounces
orange juice	3 ounces
iced tea	3 ounces

Shake with ice. Strain over ice cubes in a highball glass. Garnish with an orange slice and a mint sprig.

23. BOURBON AND BITTERS

Benchmark Sour Mash Premium Bourbon	2 ounces
simple syrup (page 59)	1 teaspoon
bitters	1–2 dashes

Shake with ice. Strain into chilled cocktail glass.

24. BOURBON AND BRANCH

Benchmark Sour Mash Premium Bourbon 1½ *ounces*
Natural spring water

Pour Bourbon over ice cubes in a highball glass. Fill with natural spring water. Stir.

25. BOURBON AND COFFEE

Benchmark Sour Mash Premium Bourbon 1 *ounce*
coffee, hot or cold
sugar
cream

Add Bourbon to cup or glass, and fill with hot or iced coffee. Stir in sugar and cream to taste.

26. BOURBON COLLINS

Benchmark Sour Mash Premium Bourbon 2 *ounces*
sugar 1 *teaspoon*
lemon juice ½ *ounce*
club soda

Shake Bourbon, sugar, and lemon juice with ice. Strain over crushed ice in a tall 12-to-14-ounce glass. Fill with club soda. Stir. Garnish with a lemon slice.

27. BOURBON DAISY

Benchmark Sour Mash Premium Bourbon 1½ *ounces*
Leroux Grenadine 1 *teaspoon*
lemon juice ½ *ounce*
club soda

Shake Bourbon, grenadine, and lemon juice with ice. Strain over ice in a wine goblet. Fill with club soda. Stir. Garnish with an orange slice and a pineapple stick.

28. BOURBON FIZZ

Benchmark Sour Mash Premium Bourbon   *1½ ounces*
lemon juice   *½ ounce*
sugar   *1 teaspoon*
club soda

Shake Bourbon, lemon juice, and sugar with ice. Strain over ice cubes in a highball glass. Fill with soda. Garnish with a lemon slice.

29. BOURBON HIGHBALL

Benchmark Sour Mash Premium Bourbon   *1½ ounces*
club soda or ginger ale

Pour Bourbon over ice cubes in a highball glass. Fill with soda. Stir.

30. BOURBON LANCER

Benchmark Sour Mash Premium Bourbon   *1½ ounces*
sugar   *½ teaspoon*
bitters   *1–2 dashes*
Champagne, chilled

Stir Bourbon, sugar, and bitters in a wine goblet. Add ice cubes and fill with chilled champagne. Garnish with a lemon twist.

31. BOURBON MANHATTAN

Benchmark Sour Mash Premium Bourbon	*1½ ounces*
Paul Masson Sweet Vermouth	*½ ounce*
bitters	*1 dash*

Stir with ice. Strain into a chilled cocktail glass. Garnish with a Maraschino cherry.

See MANHATTAN, No. 110, and variations.

32. BOURBON MIST

Benchmark Sour Mash Premium Bourbon	*1½ ounces*

Pour into an Old-Fashioned glass filled with shaved ice. Garnish with a lemon twist. Serve with short straws.

33. BOURBON RICKEY

Benchmark Sour Mash Premium Bourbon	*1½ ounces*
lime	*½*
club soda	

Pour Bourbon over ice in a highball glass. Squeeze lime over drink and drop into glass. Add soda to fill. Stir.

34. BOURBON SMASH

sugar	*1 teaspoon*
mint	*2 sprigs*
water	*½ teaspoon*
Benchmark Sour Mash Premium Bourbon	*1½ ounces*
club soda	

Muddle sugar with mint and water. Add ice cubes or shaved ice and pour in Bourbon. Top with soda. Stir.

35. BOURBON SOUR

Benchmark Sour Mash Premium Bourbon	1½ ounces
lemon juice	½ ounce
sugar	½ teaspoon

Shake with ice. Strain into a chilled sour glass. Garnish with a lemon slice and Maraschino cherry.

36. BOURBON SWIZZLE

Benchmark Sour Mash Premium Bourbon	2 ounces
lime juice	½ ounce
sugar	1 teaspoon
bitters	2–3 dashes
shaved ice	⅔ cup
club soda	

Blend together Bourbon, lime juice, sugar, bitters, and ice in a blender for 10 seconds. Pour into a highball glass. Top with club soda. Garnish with a lime twist.

37. BOURBON AND ICED TEA

Benchmark Sour Mash Premium Bourbon	1½ ounces
iced tea	
superfine sugar	

Pour Bourbon over ice cubes in a tall glass. Fill with iced tea. Add sugar to taste. Garnish with lemon slice.

38. BOURBON TEA

Benchmark Sour Mash Premium Bourbon	1 *ounce*
sugar	1 *teaspoon*
lemon	1 *slice*
cloves	2
hot tea	

Add Bourbon, sugar, lemon, and cloves to a small mug. Fill with hot tea. Stir.

39. BOURBON TODDY

Benchmark Sour Mash Premium Bourbon	1½ *ounces*
sugar	1 *teaspoon*
lemon	1 *slice*
cloves	2
boiling water	

Add Bourbon, sugar, lemon slice, and cloves to an Old-Fashioned glass. Fill with boiling water. Stir.

Variations:
   HOT TODDY (MYERS'S RUM), No. 99
   V.O. TODDY, No. 200

40. BOURBON WARD EIGHT

Benchmark Sour Mash Premium Bourbon	1½ *ounces*
lemon juice	½ *ounce*
Leroux Grenadine	½ *teaspoon*
orange bitters	1 *dash*

Shake with ice. Strain into a wine goblet or highball glass filled with crushed ice. Garnish with lemon slice, orange slice, and Maraschino cherry.

41. BOURBON AND WATER

Benchmark Sour Mash Premium Bourbon   1½ *ounces*
water

Pour Bourbon over ice cubes in a highball glass. Fill with water. Stir.

42. BOXCAR

Seagram's Extra Dry Gin	1 *ounce*
Leroux Triple Sec	1 *ounce*
lime juice	1 *teaspoon*
Leroux Grenadine	1–2 *dashes*
egg white	1

Shake very well with ice. Strain into a chilled cocktail glass that has been rimmed with sugar.

43. BRONX

Seagram's Extra Dry Gin	1½ *ounces*
dry vermouth	½ *ounce*
orange juice	½ *ounce*

Shake with ice. Strain into a chilled cocktail glass.

44. BROWN DERBY

Myers's Rum	1½ *ounces*
lime juice	½ *ounce*
maple syrup	1 *teaspoon*

Shake well with ice. Strain over ice cubes in an Old-Fashioned glass. Garnish with a lime slice.

45. BULLSHOT

Wolfschmidt Vodka	1½ ounces
lemon juice	1 teaspoon
Worcestershire sauce	3–4 drops
Tabasco sauce	1 dash
Beef bouillon, chilled	

Pour vodka, lemon juice, Worcestershire, and Tabasco over ice cubes in an Old-Fashioned glass. Fill with bouillon. Stir.

46. CAFE 7

Seagram's 7 Crown	1½ ounces
hot coffee	
whipped cream	

Pour Seagram's 7 into a cup or stemmed glass. Fill to ¼ inch of top with strong black coffee. Float a spoonful of whipped cream on top.

47. CANADIAN AND BITTERS

Seagram's V.O.	2 ounces
sugar syrup	1 teaspoon
bitters	1–2 dashes

Shake with ice. Strain into a chilled cocktail glass, or over ice cubes in an Old-Fashioned glass.

48. CANADIAN BLACKBERRY FIZZ

Seagram's V.O.	1½ ounces
Leroux Blackberry Flavored Brandy	½ ounce
sugar	½ teaspoon
lemon juice	½ ounce
club soda	

Shake V.O., blackberry flavored brandy, sugar, and lemon juice with ice. Strain into a tall glass filled with crushed ice. Top with club soda. Garnish: lemon slice.

49. CANADIAN BULLDOG

Seagram's V.O.	1 ounce
Leroux Crème de Café	1 ounce
light cream	2 ounces

Shake well with ice. Strain into an Old-Fashioned glass filled with shaved ice.

50. CANADIAN SOUR

Seagram's V.O.	1½ ounces
lemon juice	½ ounce
sugar	½ teaspoon

Shake with ice. Strain into a chilled sour glass. Garnish with a lemon slice and a Maraschino cherry.

51. CAPE CODDER

Wolfschmidt Vodka	1½ ounces
lemon or lime juice	½ ounce
cranberry juice	

Pour vodka and lemon or lime juice over ice cubes in a highball glass. Fill with cranberry juice. Stir. Garnish with an orange slice.

52. CARIBBEAN COOLER

Myers's Rum	1½ ounces
Leroux Apricot Flavored Brandy	½ ounce
cream of coconut	1 ounce
heavy cream	1 ounce
crushed ice	1 cup

Whirl in a blender at low speed for 10–15 seconds. Pour into a champagne glass or wine goblet. Garnish with a sprinkling of grated coconut and a Maraschino cherry.

53. CHERRY SOUR

Seagram's 7 Crown	¾ ounce
Leroux Cherry Flavored Brandy	¾ ounce
orange juice	1 ounce
lemon juice	½ ounce
sugar	½ teaspoon

Shake with ice. Strain into a chilled sour glass. Garnish with a lemon slice and a Maraschino cherry.

54. CLAMDIGGER

Wolfschmidt Vodka	1½ ounces
clam juice	3 ounces
tomato juice	3 ounces
Tabasco sauce	1 dash

Pour over ice cubes in a highball glass. Stir.

55. CHRISTOPHE

Myers's Rum	1 ounce
Seagram's Extra Dry Gin	½ ounce

| lime juice | 1 teaspoon |
| simple syrup | ½ teaspoon |

Shake with ice. Strain into a chilled cocktail glass. Garnish with a lime twist.

56. CLIQUET

Benchmark Sour Mash Premium Bourbon	1½ ounces
Myers's Rum	1 dash
orange juice	3 ounces

Pour over ice in a large Old-Fashioned glass. Stir. Garnish with an orange twist.

57. COBBLER

Wolfschmidt Vodka	2 ounces
Leroux Curaçao	3–4 dashes
lemon juice	1–2 dashes
Garnish: 1 slice each lemon and orange,	
1 Maraschino cherry	

Fill a large goblet with shaved ice. Add Wolfschmidt, Curaçao, and lemon juice. Stir. Garnish with fruit.

COLLINS—Collins are very tall drinks made with gin or other liquor, combined with lemon or lime juice and sugar in a tall 12-to-14-ounce glass filled with ice. The drink is topped with club soda and garnished with fruit.

BOURBON COLLINS	26
RUM COLLINS	141
SINGAPORE COLLINS	167
TOM COLLINS	183
VODKA COLLINS	187

58. COWBOY

| Seagram's 7 Crown | 1½ ounces |
| light cream | ¾ ounce |

Shake with ice. Strain into a chilled cocktail glass.

59. CROWN ROYAL MIST

| Crown Royal | 1½ ounces |

Pour into an Old-Fashioned glass filled with shaved ice. Garnish with a lemon twist. Serve with short straws.

60. CROWN ROYAL NEAT

| Crown Royal | 1½ ounces |

Pour into a brandy snifter or whisky glass. Sip slowly.

61. CROWN ROYAL AND SODA

| Crown Royal | 1½ ounces |
| club soda | |

Pour Crown Royal over ice cubes in a highball glass. Fill with club soda. Stir.

62. CROWN ROYAL AND WATER

| Crown Royal | 1½ ounces |
| water | |

Pour Crown Royal over ice cubes in a highball glass. Fill with water. Stir.

63. DAIQUIRI

Myers's Rum	*1½ ounces*
lime juice	*½ ounce*
sugar	*½ teaspoon*
bitters	*1 dash*

Shake with ice. Strain into a chilled cocktail glass.

Daiquiri Variations:

64. DAIQUIRI DELUXE

Myers's Rum	*1½ ounces*
Leroux Banana Liqueur	*½ ounce*
lime juice	*½ ounce*
sugar	*½ teaspoon*

Shake with ice. Strain into a chilled cocktail glass.

65. DAIQUIRI—FROZEN

Myers's Rum	*1½ ounces*
lime juice	*½ ounce*
sugar	*½ teaspoon*
crushed ice	*½ cup*

Blend rum, lime juice, and sugar in a blender with crushed ice for 10 to 15 seconds, until smooth. Pour into champagne glass or wine goblet. Garnish with lime slice.

66. DAISY

Seagram's Extra Dry Gin	1½ ounces
lemon juice	½ ounce
raspberry syrup	1 teaspoon
club soda	

Shake gin, lemon juice, and raspberry syrup with ice. Strain over ice in a wine goblet. Fill with club soda. Stir. Garnish with a fresh raspberry or a lemon twist.

67. DERBY

| Seagram's Extra Dry Gin | 1½ ounces |
| Leroux Peach Flavored Brandy | ½ ounce |

Shake with ice. Strain over shaved ice in a wine glass or champagne glass. Garnish with a mint sprig.

68. DIXIE WHISKEY

Benchmark Sour Mash Premium Bourbon	1½ ounces
lemon juice	1 teaspoon
powdered sugar	½ teaspoon
Leroux White Crème de Menthe	1 dash
Leroux Curaçao	1 dash

Shake with ice. Strain over ice in an Old-Fashioned glass. Garnish with a mint sprig.

69. EARTHQUAKE

Myers's Rum	½ ounce
Seagram's Extra Dry Gin	½ ounce
Leroux Abisante	½ ounce

Shake with ice. Strain into a chilled cocktail glass.

70. EGGNOG

Benchmark Sour Mash Premium Bourbon   1½ ounces
dairy eggnog, chilled

Pour Bourbon into a small glass or a mug. Fill with dairy eggnog. Sprinkle with nutmeg.

EGGNOG PUNCH—See Chapter 15

71. EL DIABLO

Olmeca Tequila   1½ ounces
Leroux Crème de Cassis   ½ ounce
lime juice   1½ teaspoons
ginger ale

Pour tequila, cassis, and lime juice over ice in a tall glass. Fill with ginger ale. Stir. Garnish with a lime wedge.

72. EMERALD COOLER

Seagram's Extra Dry Gin   1 ounce
Leroux Green Crème de Menthe   ½ ounce
sweetened lemon juice   1 ounce
club soda

Pour gin, crème de menthe, and sweetened lemon juice over ice in a highball glass. Fill with club soda. Stir. Garnish with a lemon twist.

73. FIRECRACKER

Seagram's 7 Crown   1½ ounces
cranberry juice

Pour Seagram's 7 Crown over ice cubes in a highball glass. Fill with cranberry juice. Stir. Garnish with a lemon twist.

FIZZES—Fizzes are cool drinks containing liquor, citrus juice, and sugar, poured over ice in a highball or other tall glass and "fizzed" with club soda. They may contain cordials. Golden Fizz includes egg yolk.

BOURBON FIZZ	28
BLACKBERRY FIZZ	48
GIN FIZZ	83
GOLDEN FIZZ	91
RAMOZ FIZZ	134
VODKA FIZZ	188

74. FLORIDA PUNCH

Myers's Rum	1½ ounces
Leroux Deluxe Brandy	½ ounce
grapefruit juice	1 ounce
orange juice	1 ounce

Shake with ice. Strain into a highball glass filled with crushed ice. Garnish with an orange slice.

75. FLORIDITA SPECIAL

Myers's Rum	1½ ounces
Leroux Maraschino Liqueur	½ ounce
sugar	½ teaspoon
grapefruit juice	½ teaspoon
lime juice	1 teaspoon
crushed ice	¾ cup

Blend at high speed in a blender, until smooth. Pour into wine goblet. Garnish with a Maraschino cherry.

76. FOX TROT

Myers's Rum	1½ ounces
Leroux Curaçao	1 dash
lemon juice or lime juice	2 teaspoons
sugar	½ teaspoon

Shake with ice. Strain into a chilled cocktail glass.

77. FRENCH ROSE

Seagram's Extra Dry Gin	1 ounce
Leroux Cherry Flavored Brandy	½ ounce
Leroux Cherry Liqueur	½ ounce

Shake with ice. Strain into a chilled cocktail glass.

78. FRENCH 75

Seagram's Extra Dry Gin	1½ ounces
lemon juice	½ ounce
powdered sugar	½ teaspoon
Champagne, chilled	

Shake gin, lemon juice, and sugar with ice. Strain into a wine glass. Fill with chilled Champagne.

79. GIBSON

A Gibson is a Martini (see No. 114) garnished with a cocktail onion. For a Vodka Gibson, see No. 190.

80. GIMLET

Seagram's Extra Dry Gin	2 ounces
Rose's Lime Juice	½ ounce

Shake with ice. Strain into a chilled cocktail glass.

For a VODKA GIMLET, see No. 191.

81. GIN AND BERRIES

Seagram's Extra Dry Gin	1½ ounces
Leroux Strawberry Liqueur	½ ounce
frozen strawberries, with juice	2 ounces
lemon juice	½ teaspoon
crushed ice	¼ cup
club soda	

Blend gin, strawberry liqueur, berries, lemon juice, and ice in a blender at low speed for 15 seconds. Pour into a champagne glass. Top with a splash of club soda. Garnish with a fresh strawberry.

82. GIN BUCK

Seagram's Extra Dry Gin	1½ ounces
lime juice	1 teaspoon
ginger ale	

Pour gin and lime juice over ice cubes in a highball glass. Fill with ginger ale. Stir. Garnish with a lime twist.

83. GIN FIZZ

Seagram's Extra Dry Gin	2 ounces
lemon juice	½ ounce
lime juice	½ ounce
sugar	2 teaspoons
club soda	

Shake gin, lemon juice, lime juice, and sugar with ice. Strain over ice cubes in a tall glass. Fill with club soda. Stir. Garnish with a lemon slice.

84. GIN FLIP

Seagram's Extra Dry Gin	1½ ounces
Leroux Curaçao	½ ounce
bitters	1 dash
simple syrup	1 teaspoon
small egg	1

Shake very well with ice, or blend in a blender at low speed for 5 to 10 seconds. Strain into a sour glass. Garnish with an orange twist.

85. GIN AND GINGER

Seagram's Extra Dry Gin	1½ ounces
ginger ale	

Pour gin over ice in a highball glass. Fill with ginger ale. Stir.

86. GIN AND IT

Seagram's Extra Dry Gin	1½ ounces
Paul Masson Sweet Vermouth	½ ounce

Stir with ice. Strain into a chilled cocktail glass. Or serve at room temperature, English style.

87. GIN RICKEY

Seagram's Extra Dry Gin	1½ ounces
lime	½
sugar syrup	1 teaspoon
club soda	

Pour gin over ice in a highball glass. Squeeze lime over drink and drop into glass. Add sugar syrup soda to fill. Stir.

88. GIN AND SIN

Seagram's Extra Dry Gin	1½ ounces
orange juice	¼ ounce
lemon juice	¼ ounce
Leroux Grenadine	2 dashes

Shake with ice. Strain into a chilled cocktail glass.

89. GIN SLING

Seagram's Extra Dry Gin	1½ ounces
lemon juice	¾ ounce
sugar syrup	1 teaspoon
bitters	1–2 dashes
club soda	

Shake gin, lemon juice, sugar syrup, and bitters with ice. Strain into a highball glass filled with ice. Fill with club soda. Garnish with an orange twist.

90. GIN AND TONIC (The Sgt.)

Seagram's Extra Dry Gin	1½ ounces
tonic water	

Pour gin over ice in a highball glass. Fill with tonic water. Squeeze lime wedge over drink and drop into glass. Stir.

91. GOLDEN FIZZ

Seagram's Extra Dry Gin	1½ ounces
lemon juice	½ ounce
sugar	1 teaspoon
egg yolk	1
club soda	

Shake very well with ice. Strain over ice cubes in a highball glass. Fill with club soda. Stir.

92. GOLDEN GLOW

Benchmark Sour Mash Premium Bourbon	1½ *ounces*
Myers's Rum	1 *dash*
orange juice	1 *ounce*
lemon juice	½ *ounce*
sugar	1 *teaspoon*
Leroux Grenadine	3–4 *drops*

Shake Bourbon, rum, juices, and sugar with ice. Add grenadine to the bottom of a champagne glass and strain in cocktail.

93. GREEN DRAGON

Seagram's Extra Dry Gin	1 *ounce*
Leroux Green Crème de Menthe	¾ *ounce*
Leroux Kümmel	¼ *ounce*
lemon juice	¼ *ounce*
orange bitters	1–2 *dashes*

Shake with ice. Strain over ice cubes in an Old-Fashioned glass.

94. GROG

Myers's Rum	1½ *ounces*
lemon juice	2 *teaspoons*
sugar	1 *teaspoon*
whole cloves	2
cinnamon stick	1
boiling water	

Combine rum, lemon juice, sugar, and spices in a mug. Fill with boiling water. Stir. Garnish with a lemon twist.

95. HORSE'S NECK

Seagram's 7 Crown   1½ ounces
bitters   1 dash
rind of 1 lemon, peeled in a spiral
ginger ale

Add Seagram's 7, bitters, and lemon spiral to a highball glass with ice cubes. Fill with ginger ale. Stir.

96. HOT APPLE KNOCKER

Benchmark Sour Mash Premium Bourbon
   or Myers's Rum   1½ ounces
Leroux Triple Sec   ½ ounce
hot apple cider

Pour Bourbon or rum into a heatproof glass or mug. Add triple sec. Fill with hot apple cider. Float an orange slice studded with cloves on top.

97. HOT BUTTERED RUM

Myers's Rum   1½ ounces
bitters   1 dash
sugar   1 teaspoon
butter   1 teaspoon
cloves
hot water

Add rum, bitters, sugar, butter, and cloves to a mug or thick glass. Fill with hot water. Stir.

98. HOT TODDY.

Myers's Rum   1½ ounces
sugar   1 teaspoon
very hot water   3 ounces

Combine in an Old-Fashioned glass and stir to dissolve the sugar. Garnish with a lemon or lime slice and sprinkle with a pinch of cinnamon.

Variations:
BOURBON TODDY, No. 38
V.O. TODDY, No. 200

99. HURRICANE COCKTAIL

Seagram's Extra Dry Gin	½ ounce
Seagram's V.O.	½ ounce
Leroux White Crème de Menthe	½ ounce
lemon juice	1 ounce

Shake with ice. Strain into a chilled cocktail glass.

100. HURRICANE PUNCH

Myers's Rum	1½ ounces
passion fruit syrup	½ ounce
lime juice	2 teaspoons

Shake with ice. Strain over ice in an Old-Fashioned glass. Garnish with lime slice.

101. INK STREET

Seagram's 7 Crown	1½ ounces
orange juice	¾ ounce
lemon juice	¾ ounce

Shake with ice. Strain into a chilled cocktail glass. Garnish with an orange twist.

102. ITALIAN SOOTHER

Seagram's Extra Dry Gin	*1 ounce*
Leroux Amaretto di Torino	*1 ounce*
half and half	*4 ounces*

Shake well with ice. Strain into an Old-Fashioned glass filled with shaved ice. Garnish with an orange slice.

103. JOLLY ROGER

Myers's Rum	*1 ounce*
Leroux Banana Liqueur	*1 ounce*
sweetened lemon juice	*2 ounces*

Shake with ice. Strain over ice cubes in a wine goblet.

104. KIR GIN COCKTAIL

Seagram's Extra Dry Gin	*1½ ounces*
Leroux Crème de Cassis	*2 teaspoons*
club soda	

Pour gin and cassis over ice cubes in a wine goblet. Fill with club soda. Stir. Garnish with a lemon twist.

105. LICORICE SLUSH

Wolfschmidt Vodka	*1 ounce*
Leroux Anisette	*1½ ounces*
lemon sherbet	*1 scoop*

Blend in a blender until slushy. Pour into a tall, narrow highball glass. Garnish with licorice stick or mint sprig.

106. LINSTEAD COCKTAIL

Seagram's V.O.	1½ ounces
sweetened pineapple juice	1½ ounces
bitters	1 dash

Shake with ice. Strain into a chilled cocktail glass. Garnish with a lemon twist.

107. LONG ISLAND TEA

Seagram's 7 Crown	½ ounce
Seagram's Extra Dry Gin	½ ounce
Myers's Rum	½ ounce
Wolfschmidt Vodka	½ ounce
sweetened lemon juice	2 ounces
cola drink	

Pour liquors over ice cubes in a tall, slender glass. Add lemon juice and fill with cola. Stir well.

108. MAI TAI

Myers's Rum	1½ ounces
Leroux Curaçao	½ ounce
lime juice	½ ounce
Leroux Crème de Noya	1 teaspoon
sugar	1 teaspoon

Shake with ice. Strain over ice in a highball glass. Garnish with lime slice, pineapple stick, and mint sprig.

109. MANHATTAN

Seagram's 7 Crown	1½ ounces
Paul Masson Sweet Vermouth	½ ounce
bitters	1 dash

Stir with ice. Strain into chilled cocktail glass. Garnish with a Maraschino cherry.

110. DRY MANHATTAN

Seagram's 7 Crown	1½ ounces
Paul Masson Double Dry Vermouth	½ ounce
bitters	1 dash

Stir with ice. Strain into a chilled cocktail glass. Garnish with a Maraschino Cherry.

111. PERFECT MANHATTAN

Seagram's 7 Crown	1½ ounces
Paul Masson Double Dry Vermouth	2 teaspoons
Paul Masson Sweet Vermouth	1 teaspoon
bitters	1 dash

Stir with ice. Strain into a chilled cocktail glass. Garnish with a Maraschino Cherry.

For a BOURBON MANHATTAN, see No. 31. A ROB ROY is a SCOTCH MANHATTAN, see Nos. 137–39.

112. MAPLE 7 SOUR

Seagram's 7 Crown	1½ ounces
lemon juice	½ ounce
maple syrup	1 teaspoon

Shake with ice. Strain into a chilled sour glass. Garnish with a lemon slice and Maraschino cherry.

113. MARGARITA

Olmeca Tequila	1½ ounces
Leroux Triple Sec	½ ounce
lime juice	½ ounce
coarse salt	

Shake tequila, triple sec, and lime juice with ice. Dip rim of chilled cocktail glass in lime juice, then in coarse salt to coat. Strain drink into glass.

114. MARTINI

Seagram's Extra Dry Gin	1½ ounces
Paul Masson Double Dry Vermouth	½ ounce

Stir with ice. Strain into a chilled cocktail glass. Garnish with an olive.

115. EXTRA DRY MARTINI, AND OTHER VARIATIONS

Seagram's Extra Dry Gin	2 ounces
Paul Masson Double Dry Vermouth	1 dash

Stir with ice. Strain into a chilled cocktail glass or over rocks in an Old-Fashioned glass. Garnish with a lemon twist.

Variations:
Vary the proportions of Seagram's Extra Dry Gin and Paul Masson Double Dry Vermouth to taste. Serve straight up or on the rocks, or blended to a slush with crushed ice for a frosty variation. Add a dash or two of Angostura or orange bitters before stirring. Garnish with your choice of olive (stuffed with pimiento or almond),

rolled anchovy with caper, pickled mushroom, or twist of lemon or orange. A Gibson is a martini garnished with a small cocktail onion.

For a VODKA MARTINI, see No. 192.

116. MATADOR

Olmeca Tequila	*1 ounce*
pineapple juice	*2 ounces*
lime juice	*½ ounce*

Shake with ice. Strain over ice cubes in an Old-Fashioned glass. Garnish with a lime slice.
For a Frozen Matador, increase Tequila to 1½ ounces, blend all ingredients with ⅜ cup crushed ice in a blender, and pour into a wine glass. Garnish: pineapple stick.

117. MINT JULEP

simple syrup	*1 teaspoon*
mint	*4 sprigs*
Benchmark Sour Mash Premium Bourbon	*2 ounces*

In a tall glass or julep mug, muddle simple syrup with mint leaves. Fill glass with shaved ice and pour in Bourbon. Stir. Again fill with shaved ice (some will melt when Bourbon is poured in). Garnish with additional mint sprig.

118. MOSCOW MULE

Wolfschmidt Vodka	*1½ ounces*
lime	*½*
ginger beer	

Pour vodka over ice in a highball glass. Squeeze lime over drink and drop into glass. Fill with ginger beer. Stir.

119. NEGRONI

Seagram's Extra Dry Gin	1 ounce
Paul Masson Sweet Vermouth	1 ounce
Campari	1 ounce

Shake with ice. Strain into chilled cocktail glass. Garnish with lemon twist.

120. NEW YORKER

Seagram's 7 Crown	1½ ounces
lime juice	½ ounce
Leroux Grenadine	¼ teaspoon
sugar	½ teaspoon

Shake with ice. Strain over ice cubes in an Old-Fashioned glass. Garnish with an orange twist.

121. NINOTCHKA

Wolfschmidt Vodka	1½ ounces
Leroux White Crème de Cacao	2 teaspoons
lemon juice	2 teaspoons

Shake with ice. Strain over ice cubes in an Old-Fashioned glass.

122. OLD-FASHIONED

sugar	1 teaspoon
bitters	1 dash
water	1 teaspoon
Seagram's 7 Crown	1½ ounces

Muddle sugar with bitters and water. Add ice cubes and pour in Seagram's 7 Crown. Stir. Garnish with lemon twist, orange slice, and Maraschino cherry.

Variations:
V.O. OLD-FASHIONED, No. 197
SCOTCH OLD-FASHIONED, No. 154

123. ORANGE BLOSSOM

Seagram's Extra Dry Gin	*1½ ounces*
orange juice	*1 ounce*

Shake with ice. Strain into a chilled cocktail glass rimmed with sugar. Garnish with an orange slice.

124. PALL MALL

Seagram's Extra Dry Gin	*¾ ounce*
Paul Masson Double Dry Vermouth	*¾ ounce*
Paul Masson Sweet Vermouth	*¾ ounce*
Leroux White Crème de Menthe	*1 teaspoon*
orange bitters	*1 dash*

Stir with ice. Strain over ice cubes in an Old-Fashioned glass.

125. PANAMA

Myers's Rum	*1 ounce*
Leroux Crème de Cacao	*½ ounce*
light cream	*½ ounce*

Shake with ice. Strain over ice cubes in an Old-Fashioned glass. Garnish with a sprinkle of nutmeg.

126. PARISIAN

Seagram's Extra Dry Gin	¾ ounce
Paul Masson Double Dry Vermouth	¾ ounce
Leroux Crème de Cassis	¾ ounce

Shake with ice. Strain into a chilled cocktail glass.

127. PEACH DAIQUIRI

Myers's Rum	1½ ounces
Leroux Peach Liqueur	½ ounce
peach, fresh, frozen, or canned	½
lime juice	½ ounce
crushed ice	⅓ cup

Blend all ingredients in a blender for 10–15 seconds. Pour into a chilled champagne glass.

128. PINA COLADA

Myers's Rum	1½ ounces
creme of coconut (from can)	1 ounce
pineapple juice	2 ounces
crushed ice	½ cup

Blend in a blender at low speed for 10–15 seconds. Pour into a champagne glass or highball glass. Garnish with a pineapple stick and a Maraschino cherry.

One Step: Use Party Tyme Piña Colada Mix as directed.

129. PINEAPPLE DAIQUIRI

Myers's Rum	1½ ounces
pineapple juice	1½ ounces
crushed pineapple	¼ cup
lime juice	½ ounce
sugar	1 teaspoon
crushed ice	⅔ cup

Blend together in a blender at low speed for 15 seconds. Pour into a chilled champagne glass or wine goblet. Garnish with a pineapple stick.

130. PINK LADY

Seagram's Extra Dry Gin	1½ ounces
lemon juice	¾ ounce
Leroux Grenadine	½ ounce
egg white	1

Shake very well with ice. Strain into a chilled cocktail glass.

131. PLANTER'S PUNCH

Myers's Rum	1½ ounces
orange juice	3 ounces
lemon or lime juice	½ ounce
sugar	1 teaspoon
Leroux Grenadine	1 dash

Shake with ice. Strain over ice in a highball or tall 12-to-14-ounce glass. Garnish with an orange slice and a Maraschino cherry.

132. POLO

Seagram's Extra Dry Gin	1½ ounces
orange juice	2 teaspoons
graperfruit juice	2 teaspoons

Shake with ice. Strain over ice in an Old-Fashioned glass.

133. PURPLE PASSION

Wolfschmidt Vodka	1½ ounces
grape juice	

Pour vodka over ice in a highball glass. Fill with grape juice. Stir.

134. RAMOZ FIZZ

Seagram's Extra Dry Gin	2 ounces
lemon juice	½ ounce
lime juice	¼ ounce
cream	½ ounce
egg white	1
orange flower water (optional)	2 dashes
crushed ice	1 cup
club soda	

Blend gin, juices, cream, egg white, orange flower water, and ice at high speed for 5 seconds. Pour into a tall 14-ounce glass and fill with club soda. Stir gently.

135. RASPBERRY COOLER

Wolfschmidt Vodka	1½ ounces
raspberry sherbet	1 scoop
Leroux Crème de Cassis	1 ounce
light cream	1 ounce

Whirl at low speed in a blender for 15 seconds. Pour into a champagne glass or wine goblet. Garnish with a raspberry and a mint sprig.

136. RED BARON

Seagram's Extra Dry Gin	2 ounces
Leroux Grenadine	1 ounce
orange juice	

Pour gin and grenadine over ice cubes in a highball glass. Fill with orange juice. Stir. Garnish with an orange slice.

RICKEYS—Similar to Collins and Fizzes, Rickeys are made with liquor, lime juice, and club soda. They are generally unsweetened and served with the lime rind in the glass.

BOURBON RICKEY	33
GIN RICKEY	88
RUM RICKEY	145
TEQUILA RICKEY	176

137. ROB ROY

The Famous Grouse Scotch	1½ ounces
Paul Masson Sweet Vermouth	½ ounce
bitters	1 dash

Stir with ice. Strain into a chilled cocktail glass. Garnish with a Maraschino cherry.

138. DRY ROB ROY

The Famous Grouse Scotch	1½ ounces
Paul Masson Double Dry Vermouth	½ ounce
bitters	1 dash

Stir with ice. Strain into a chilled cocktail glass. Garnish with a lemon twist.

139. PERFECT ROB ROY

The Famous Grouse Scotch	1½ ounces
Paul Masson Double Dry Vermouth	2 teaspoons
Paul Masson Sweet Vermouth	1 teaspoon
bitters	1 dash

Stir with ice. Strain into a chilled cocktail glass. Garnish with a Maraschino cherry.

140. RUM AND COLA

| Myers's Rum | 1½ ounces |
| cola | |

Pour rum over ice cubes in a highball glass. Fill with cola. Stir.

141. RUM COLLINS

Myers's Rum	2 ounces
sugar	1 teaspoon
lime juice	½ ounce
club soda	

Shake rum, sugar, and lime juice with ice. Strain over crushed ice in a tall 12-to-14-ounce glass. Fill with club soda. Stir. Garnish with a lime slice.

142. RUM AND FRUIT COOLER

Myers's Rum	2 ounces
orange and lime	2 slices each
sugar	1 teaspoon
Leroux Curaçao	½ ounce
lemon-lime soda	

Muddle fruit slices with rum, sugar, and Curaçao in the bottom of a tall glass. Add ice cubes and fill with lemon-lime soda. Stir. Garnish with a Maraschino cherry.

143. RUM AND GINGER

| Myers's Rum | 1½ ounces |
| ginger ale | |

Pour rum over ice cubes in a highball glass. Fill with ginger ale. Stir. Garnish with a lime wedge.

144. RUM JULEP

simple syrup	1 teaspoon
mint	2 sprigs
Myers's Rum	2 ounces
club soda (optional)	

In a tall glass, muddle sugar syrup with mint leaves. Fill glass with shaved ice and pour in rum. Stir. Add more shaved ice as necessary and top with club soda if desired. Garnish with additional mint sprig.

145. RUM RICKEY

Myers's Rum	1½ ounces
lime	½
club soda	

Pour rum over ice in a highball glass. Squeeze lime over drink and drop into glass. Add soda to fill. Stir.

146. RUSSIAN BEAR

Wolfschmidt Vodka	1 ounce
Leroux White Crème de Cacao	½ ounce
heavy cream	½ ounce

Shake with ice. Strain into a chilled cocktail glass.

147. RUSTY FAMOUS GROUSE

The Famous Grouse Scotch	¾ ounce
Lochan Ora	

Pour over ice in an Old-Fashioned glass and stir. Or serve without ice in a cocktail glass.

148. SALTY DOG

Wolfschmidt Vodka	1½ ounces
grapefruit juice	
salt (optional)	

Pour vodka over ice in a highball glass. Fill with grapefruit juice. Stir. If desired, sprinkle with coarse salt to taste.

149. SANGRITA

Olmeca Tequila	1 ounce
orange, lemon, lime	1 slice each
sangria wine	

Stir tequila with fruit slices in a tall glass. Add ice cubes and fill with sangria. Stir.

150. SAZERAC

Leroux Abisante	¼ teaspoon
sugar	½ teaspoon
bitters	1 dash
water	½ ounce
Benchmark Sour Mash Premium Bourbon	2 ounces

Swirl abisante in a chilled Old-Fashioned glass to coat the sides. Add sugar, bitters, and water and muddle well. Add ice cubes and Bourbon and stir. Garnish with a lemon twist.

151. SCOTCH BUCK

The Famous Grouse Scotch	1½ ounces
lime juice	½ ounce
ginger ale	

Shake Scotch and lime juice with ice. Strain over ice in a highball glass. Fill with ginger ale. Stir. Garnish with a lime slice.

152. SCOTCH MIST

| *The Glenlivet Scotch* | *1½ ounces* |

Pour into an Old-Fashioned glass filled with shaved ice. Garnish with a lemon twist. Serve with short straws.

153. SCOTCH NEAT

| *The Glenlivet Scotch* | *1½ ounces* |

Pour into a whisky glass or brandy snifter. Sip.

154. SCOTCH OLD-FASHIONED

sugar	*1 teaspoon*
bitters	*1 dash*
water	*1 teaspoon*
The Famous Grouse Scotch	*1½ ounces*

Muddle sugar with bitters and water. Add ice cubes and pour in Scotch. Stir. Garnish with a lemon twist, orange slice, and Maraschino cherry.

Variations:
    OLD-FASHIONED (7 CROWN), No. 122
    V.O. OLD-FASHIONED, No. 197

155. SCOTCH ON THE ROCKS

| *The Famous Grouse Scotch* | *1½ ounces* |

Pour over ice cubes in an Old-Fashioned glass.

156. SCOTCH SMASH

sugar	1 teaspoon
mint	2 sprigs
water	½ teaspoon
The Famous Grouse Scotch	1½ ounces
club soda	

Muddle sugar, water, and mint in the bottom of a highball glass. Fill half full with shaved ice. Pour in Scotch and top with a splash of club soda. Garnish with orange, lemon, and lime slices.

157. SCOTCH AND SODA

The Famous Grouse Scotch	1½ ounces
club soda	

Pour Scotch over ice cubes in a highball glass. Fill with club soda. Stir.

158. SCOTCH SOUR

The Famous Grouse Scotch	1½ ounces
lemon juice	½ ounce
sugar	½ teaspoon

Shake with ice. Strain into a chilled sour glass. Garnish with a lemon slice and a Maraschino cherry.

159. SCOTCH SWIZZLE

The Famous Grouse Scotch	2 ounces
lime juice	½ ounce
sugar	1 teaspoon
bitters	1 dash

Pour over shaved ice in a highball glass. Stir with a swizzle stick until foamy.

160. SCOTCH AND WATER

The Glenlivet Scotch	*1½ ounces*
water	

Pour Scotch over ice cubes in a highball glass. Fill with water. Stir.

161. SCREWDRIVER

Wolfschmidt Vodka	*1½ ounces*
orange juice	

Pour vodka over ice cubes in a highball glass. Fill with orange juice. Stir.

162. SEAGRAM'S HIGH TEA

Seagram's Extra Dry Gin	*1½ ounces*
Leroux Triple Sec	*½ ounce*
lemon juice	*1 teaspoon*
sugar	*½ teaspoon*
iced tea	

Shake gin, triple sec, lemon juice, and sugar with ice. Strain over ice cubes in a highball glass. Fill with iced tea. Stir. Garnish with a lemon wedge.

163. SEAGRAM'S PINK LEMONADE

Seagram's Extra Dry Gin	*1½ ounces*
pink lemonade	

Pour gin over ice cubes in a highball glass. Fill with pink lemonade. Stir. Garnish with a lemon slice.

164. 7 & GINGER OR COLA

Seagram's 7 Crown   1½ ounces
ginger ale or cola

Pour Seagram's 7 Crown over ice cubes in a highball glass. Fill with ginger ale or cola. Stir.

165. 7 & 7

Seagram's 7 Crown   1½ ounces
7-Up

Pour Seagram's 7 Crown over ice cubes in a highball glass. Fill with lemon-lime soda. Stir.

166. SIDECAR

Seagram's Extra Dry Gin   1 ounce
Leroux Triple Sec   ½ ounce
lemon juice   ½ ounce

Shake with ice. Strain into a chilled cocktail glass. Garnish with a Maraschino cherry.

167. SINGAPORE COLLINS

Seagram's V.O.   2 ounces
sugar   1 teaspoon
lime juice   ½ ounce
club soda

Shake V.O., sugar, and lime juice with ice. Strain over crushed ice in a tall 12-to-14-ounce glass. Fill with soda. Stir. Garnish with a lime slice.

168. SKY CLUB

Seagram's 7 Crown	1½ ounces
Myers's Rum	1 dash
orange juice	3 ounces

Pour over ice in an Old-Fashioned glass. Stir. Garnish with an orange twist.

169. SOMBRERO MEXICALI

Olmeca Tequila	¾ ounce
Leroux Coffee Flavored Brandy	¾ ounce
heavy cream	1 ounce

Pour over ice cubes in an Old-Fashioned glass. Stir.

SOURS—Sours are tart, lemony cocktails made with almost any liquor plus lemon juice and sugar. They are generally served in a sour or Delmonico glass (about 4-to-6-ounce stemmed glass), garnished with a lemon slice and a cherry. *Short and easy:* Make sours with Party Tyme Freeze-Dried Whiskey Sour Cocktail Mix.

APRICOT SOUR	3
BOURBON SOUR	35
CANADIAN SOUR	50
MAPLE 7 SOUR	112
SCOTCH SOUR	158
CHERRY SOUR	53
SUNNY SOUR	173
SUNNIER SOUR	174
SUNNIEST SOUR	175
TEQUILA SOUR	177
WHISKEY SOUR	205

170. SQUALL

Myers's Rum	2 ounces
green passion fruit juice	1½ ounces
lemon juice	1 ounce
papaya juice	1 dash

Shake with ice. Strain into a tall glass filled with crushed ice. Garnish with an orange slice and a Maraschino cherry.

STINGER: See V.O. Stinger, No. 199.

171. STONE FENCE

The Famous Grouse Scotch	2 ounces
bitters	1 dash
apple cider	

Pour Scotch over ice in a tall glass and add bitters. Fill with apple cider. Stir.

172. STRAWBERRY DAIQUIRI

Myers's Rum	1½ ounces
Leroux Strawberry Liqueur	½ ounce
sliced strawberries	½ cup
lemon juice	½ ounce
sugar	1 teaspoon
crushed ice	½ cup

Whirl in a blender at low speed for 10 to 15 seconds. Pour into a chilled champagne glass. Garnish with a strawberry.

173. SUNNY SOUR

Myers's Rum	2 ounces
lemon juice	½ ounce
superfine sugar	1 teaspoon

Shake rum, lemon juice and sugar with ice until frosty. Strain into cocktail glass. Garnish with a lemon wedge and cherry.

174. SUNNIER SOUR

Myers's Rum	2 ounces
lemon juice	½ ounce
superfine sugar	1 teaspoon
chilled grapefruit juice	1½ ounces

Shake rum, lemon juice, sugar and grapefruit juice with ice until frosty. Strain over ice cubes in a highball glass. Fill with club soda. Stir. Garnish with a grapefruit wedge.

175. SUNNIEST SOUR

Myers's Rum	2 ounces
lemon juice	½ ounce
superfine sugar	1 teaspoon
orange juice	3 ounces
club soda	

Shake rum, lemon juice, sugar and orange juice with ice until frosty. Strain over ice cubes in a highball glass. Fill with club soda. Stir. Garnish with orange wedge.

176. TEQUILA RICKEY

Olmeca Tequila	1½ ounces
lime	½
club soda	

Pour tequila over ice in a highball glass. Squeeze lime over drink and drop into glass. Fill with soda. Stir.

177. TEQUILA SOUR

Olmeca Tequila	1½ ounces
lemon juice	½ ounce
sugar	½ teaspoon

Shake with ice. Strain into a chilled sour glass. Garnish with a lemon slice and a Maraschino cherry.

178. TEQUILA SUNRISE

Olmeca Tequila	1½ ounces
Leroux Grenadine	1 teaspoon
orange juice	

Pour tequila and grenadine over ice cubes in a highball glass. Fill with orange juice. Stir. Garnish with an orange slice.

179. TEQUILA SUNSTROKE

Olmeca Tequila	1½ ounces
Leroux Triple Sec	2 dashes
grapefruit juice	3 ounces

Pour over ice in an Old-Fashioned glass. Stir.

180. TEQUILA AND TEA

Olmeca Tequila   *1 ounce*
iced tea
lemon juice
sugar

Pour tequila over ice cubes in a highball glass. Fill with iced tea. Add lemon juice and sugar to taste. Stir. Garnish with a lemon wedge.

181. THISTLE

The Famous Grouse Scotch   *1 ounce*
Paul Masson Sweet Vermouth   *1 ounce*
bitters   *2 dashes*

Stir with ice. Strain into a chilled cocktail glass.

182. T 'N' T

Olmeca Tequila   *1½ ounces*
tonic water

Pour tequila over ice cubes in a highball glass. Fill with tonic. Stir. Squeeze a lime wedge over the drink and drop it in.

183. TOM COLLINS

Seagram's Extra Dry Gin   *2 ounces*
sugar   *1 teaspoon*
lemon juice   *½ ounce*
club soda

Shake gin, sugar, and lemon juice with ice. Strain over crushed ice in a tall 12-to-14-ounce glass. Fill with soda. Stir. Garnish with a lemon slice.

184. TOM AND JERRY

eggs	2
sugar	2 teaspoons
Seagram's 7 Crown or Benchmark Sour Mash Premium Bourbon	3 ounces
hot milk	

Separate eggs. Beat whites until frothy, add sugar, and beat until stiff. Beat yolks until creamy. Fold in whites. Divide egg mixture between 2 cups or mugs. Pour 1½ ounces Seagram's 7 or Benchmark Sour Mash Premium Bourbon into each mug and stir. Fill with hot milk. Makes 2 drinks.

185. UNION JACK

Myers's Rum	1½ ounces
applejack	1 ounce
sweetened lemon juice	2 ounces
Leroux Grenadine	1 teaspoon

Shake rum, applejack, and lemon juice with ice. Strain into a chilled wine glass. Float grenadine on top.

186. VALENCIA

Leroux Apricot Flavored Brandy	1 ounce
Seagram's 7 Crown	1 ounce
orange juice	1 ounce
bitters	1 dash

Shake with ice. Strain over ice cubes in an Old-Fashioned glass.

187. VODKA COLLINS

Wolfschmidt Vodka	2 ounces
sugar	1 teaspoon
lemon juice	½ ounce
club soda	

Shake vodka, sugar, and lemon juice with ice. Strain over crushed ice in a tall 12-to-14-ounce glass. Fill with soda. Stir. Garnish with a lemon slice.

188. VODKA FIZZ

Wolfschmidt Vodka	2 ounces
lemon juice	½ ounce
lime juice	½ ounce
sugar	2 teaspoons
club soda	

Shake vodka, lemon juice, lime juice, and sugar with ice. Strain over ice cubes in a tall glass. Fill with club soda. Stir. Garnish with a lemon slice.

189. VODKA FLIP

Wolfschmidt Vodka	1½ ounces
bitters	2 dashes
sugar syrup	1 teaspoon
small egg	1

Shake very well with ice, or blend in a blender at low speed for 5 to 10 seconds. Strain into a sour glass. Garnish with a sprinkle of nutmeg.

190. VODKA GIBSON

A Vodka Gibson is a Vodka Martini (see No. 192) garnished with a cocktail onion.

191. VODKA GIMLET

Wolfschmidt Vodka	*1½ ounces*
Rose's Lime Juice	*1½ ounces*

Shake with ice. Strain into a chilled cocktail glass. For Gin Gimlet, see No. 81.

192. VODKA MARTINI

Wolfschmidt Vodka	*1½ ounces*
Paul Masson Double Dry Vermouth	*½ ounce*

Stir with ice. Strain into a chilled cocktail glass. Garnish with an olive, pickled mushroom, or lemon twist.

For Dry and other Martini and Gibson variations see Nos. 114 and 115.

193. VODKA TWIST

Wolfschmidt Vodka	*1½ ounces*
cream	*1 ounce*
orange sherbet	*1 scoop*

Blend in a blender until smooth. Pour into a wine goblet or soda glass. Garnish with an orange slice.

194. VOLGA BOATMAN

Wolfschmidt Vodka	*1 ounce*
Leroux Cherry Flavored Brandy	*1 ounce*
orange juice	*1 ounce*

Shake with ice. Strain into a chilled cocktail glass, or over ice in an Old-Fashioned glass.

195. V.O. HIGHBALL

Seagram's V.O.	*1½ ounces*
mineral water, club soda, or ginger ale	

Pour whisky over ice cubes in a highball glass. Fill with mineral water, soda, or ginger ale. Stir.

196. V.O. MIST

Seagram's V.O.	*1½ ounces*

Pour into an Old-Fashioned glass filled with shaved ice. Garnish with a lemon twist. Serve with short straws.

197. V.O. OLD-FASHIONED

sugar	*1 teaspoon*
bitters	*1 dash*
water	*1 teaspoon*
Seagram's V.O.	*1½ ounces*

Muddle sugar with bitters and water. Add ice cubes and pour in whisky. Stir. Garnish with lemon twist, orange slice, and Maraschino cherry.

Variations:
>   OLD-FASHIONED (SEAGRAM'S 7 CROWN), No. 122
>   SCOTCH OLD-FASHIONED, No. 154

198. V.O. ON THE ROCKS

Seagram's V.O.   1½ ounces

Pour over ice cubes in an Old-Fashioned glass.

199. V.O. STINGER

Seagram's V.O.   1½ ounces
Leroux White Crème de Menthe   1 ounce

Stir with ice. Strain into a chilled cocktail glass or Old-Fashioned glass.

200. V.O. TODDY

Seagram's V.O.   1½ ounces
sugar   1 teaspoon
lemon   1 slice
cloves   2
boiling water

Add V.O., sugar, lemon slice, and cloves to an Old-Fashioned glass. Fill with boiling water. Stir.

Variations:
    HOT TODDY (MYERS'S RUM), No. 99
    BOURBON TODDY, No. 38

201. WALLBANGER

Wolfschmidt Vodka   1 ounce
Leroux Anisette   ½ ounce
orange juice

Pour vodka and anisette over ice cubes in a highball glass. Fill with orange juice. Stir. Garnish with an orange slice.

202. WARD EIGHT

Seagram's V.O.	1½ ounces
lemon juice	½ ounce
Leroux Grenadine	½ teaspoon
orange bitters	1 dash

Shake with ice. Strain into a highball glass or wine goblet filled with crushed ice. Garnish with a lemon slice. Serve with straws.

203. WASHINGTON NORTH

Seagram's V.O.	1 ounce
Paul Masson Double Dry Vermouth	½ ounce
sugar syrup	1-2 dashes
bitters	1-2 dashes

Shake with ice. Strain over ice cubes in an Old-Fashioned glass.

204. WATERMELON COOLER

Wolfschmidt Vodka	1½ ounces
Leroux Maraschino Liqueur	½ ounce
lime juice	½ ounce
crushed ice	¾ cup
watermelon meat	1 cup

Blend in a blender until smooth. Pour into a large goblet or tall glass. Garnish with a sprig of mint.

205. WHISKEY SOUR

Seagram's 7 Crown	1½ ounces
lemon juice	½ ounce
sugar	1 teaspoon

Shake with ice. Strain into a chilled sour glass. Garnish with a lemon slice and a Maraschino cherry.

206. WHITE ALEXANDER

Seagram's Extra Dry Gin	1 ounce
Leroux White Crème de Cacao	1 ounce
cream	1 ounce

Shake with ice. Strain into a chilled cocktail glass.

207. WHITE LADY

Seagram's Extra Dry Gin	1 ounce
Leroux Triple Sec	½ ounce
lemon juice	½ ounce
egg white	1

Shake very well with ice. Strain into a chilled cocktail glass.

208. WHITE RUSSIAN

Seagram's Extra Dry Gin	½ ounce
Wolfschmidt Vodka	½ ounce
Leroux White Crème de Menthe	½ ounce

Shake with ice. Strain into a chilled cocktail glass.

209. WHITE SCOTCH

The Famous Grouse Scotch	1½ ounces
honey	1 teaspoon
milk	4 ounces

Shake with ice until frothy. Strain over ice cubes in a highball glass.

210. WHITE SHADOW

Seagram's 7 Crown	1 ounce
Leroux Abisante	1 ounce
cream	1 ounce

Shake well with ice. Strain into a chilled cocktail glass. Sprinkle with nutmeg.

211. WIMBLEDON WHISTLE

| Seagram's Extra Dry Gin | 1½ ounces |
| Schweppes' Bitter Lemon | |

Pour gin over ice cubes in a highball glass. Fill with bitter lemon. Stir.

212. WOLF AND TONIC

| Wolfschmidt Vodka | 1½ ounces |
| tonic water | |

Pour vodka over ice in a highball glass. Fill with tonic water. Squeeze lime wedge over drink and drop into glass. Stir.

213. XYLOPHONE

Olmeca Tequila	1 ounce
Leroux White Crème de Cacao	½ ounce
sugar syrup	½ ounce
cream	1 ounce
crushed ice	½ cup

Blend at low speed in blender for 1 minute. Pour into a wine glass and top with a Maraschino cherry.

214. YELLOWBIRD

Benchmark Sour Mash Premium Bourbon	1½ ounces
Paul Masson Sweet Vermouth	½ ounce
orange juice	½ ounce
Leroux Claristine	1 dash

Shake with ice. Strain over ice cubes in an Old-Fashioned glass. Garnish with a lemon wedge.

215. ZERO MINT JULEP

Leroux Green Crème de Menthe	½ ounce
Benchmark Sour Mash Premium Bourbon	1½ ounces

Pour crème de menthe over crushed ice in an Old-Fashioned glass. Place in freezer until glass frosts over. Add Bourbon. Stir gently. Garnish with mint sprig.

216. ZOMBIE

Myers's Rum	2 ounces
Leroux Apricot Flavored Brandy	½ ounce
pineapple juice	½ ounce
papaya nectar	½ ounce
lime juice	½ ounce
sugar	½ teaspoon

Shake well with ice. Pour unstrained into a tall glass. Garnish with a pineapple stick and a Maraschino cherry.

217. SPECIALTY OF YOUR HOUSE COCKTAIL (Master Recipe)

1 jigger (1½ ounces liquor—or combination of liquors) for average-size glasses: 1 ounce for punch cup servings; 2 ounces for very tall drinks. Add dilutant juice or mixer, stir or shake very well with ice. Set off tart juice such as lemon or lime with sugar syrup, or with a sweet liqueur. Add ice to glass or shaker first. Then add liquor, sweetener, juice, and stir well. If soda or carbonated beverages are used, add these last, and stir briefly.

And remember to keep a pitcher of juice, cold mineral water, or sodas on hand for those who want to sit one out. Serve these in style, too, with ice and a twist of lemon, or other garnish.

8

Cooking with Spirits

You can bring the drama of flavoring dishes to your parties, add the elegant accent that comes from bottles you have at the bar, enjoy meats with succulent tenderness and subtle seasoning, or dip into desserts of exquisite flavor, with smooth sauces—if you learn to cook with spirits. That is why many recipes in this book call for liquor ingredients.

Liquors are more than natural sources of flavor. Here are some practical, no-nonsense techniques to take advantage of three properties of liquor valuable to cooks: to flavor, to marinate, and to preserve.

THE ART OF FLAVORING

All whiskies can be used for flavoring cooked dishes. In the process, the alcohol cooks off, leaving the flavor of the drink to season the food. The distinctive flavor of The Famous Grouse Scotch adds a subtle note to pork dishes, or to black bean soup; smooth Seagram's V.O. or Seagram's 7 Crown mellows beef roasts, the subtle tang of Seagram's Extra Dry Gin adds zest to poultry and fish dishes. Benchmark Sour Mash Premium Bourbon and Myers's Rum marry well with meats and with desserts. And of course the sweet fruity or herbal flavors of Leroux liqueurs are naturals for dessert.

Take advantage of the distillations of fine flavor in your bar bottles. A surprising dash of Benchmark Sour Mash Premium Bourbon transforms a meat loaf to party fare; mellow whisky flavors "beef up" many meat dishes. It is the juniper in gin which flavors poultry so superbly. And for proof of what liquor flavors can do for even a simple yeast dough, try a Baba au Rum, for dessert or coffee time snack (see Chapter 16).

In cooking fat meats, add liquor after meat is browned; the alcohol will help reduce fatty tissues while it flavors the meat in cooking.

MARINATING WITH LIQUOR TENDERIZES

You can be economy-minded, and produce great party fare. Marinades with a liquor base tenderize less expensive cuts of meats and poultry as they flavor. The alcohol softens tissues and imparts a bouquet of its own. How long to marinate? Long enough for flavor penetration— ½ hour to overnight, the longer the soaking, the better the flavor.

PRESERVING PARTY SPECIALTIES

Liquors also help to preserve foods. That is why the liquor added to cheese crocks helps make a blend that can be stored indefinitely. (See Chapter 9). Plum puddings or fruitcakes, your own or store bought, take on mellow flavor, moist texture—and keep well—when they are doused periodically with Myers's Rum.

*Cooking with spirits
is a naturally better
way to*
  *Flavor foods
  Tenderize meats
  Serve with style*

Cooking
with Spirit

The
Cocktail
Supper

PART 3

The Cocktail Party... And More

How to plan a cocktail party
Cocktail supplies
Stay for supper
Parties for the Two of You
Great Hors D'oeuvre
Come to Dinner

9

Come for Cocktails

The origin of the name cocktail makes interesting speculation. Some say that a Colonial American waitress used the tail feather of a cock to stir a mixed drink. Others say this comes from the name of an Aztec princess Xochitl, who is reported to have given such a drink to the King, with romantic results. Or was it a mixed drink, Coquetel, from the wine-growing district of the Gironde, that gave us this name? Whatever the source, the cocktail is now more than an aperitif drink.

A cocktail party is the most popular form of entertaining large and mixed groups. It includes food as well as drink, and in fact often now becomes a cocktail supper. A cocktail party can be pegged to any theme—seasonal, holiday, sports, business, social, or a special celebration.

THE PARTY WITH A PLUS

If there were no such thing as a cocktail party, we'd have to invent one, to satisfy current entertainment situations. We no longer require a formal social occasion to justify a party get-together. An evening of talk and drinks and some food can be its own reality—now as likely to occur at home as in a bar or club—and as likely to include as many women as men.

Our business and social lives are often intermingled.

The yen—or the need—to entertain may be stronger than the capacity for formal parties. And when the time is right for a get-together, we don't want to wait for a special date or holiday to plan the party. The answer? Come for cocktails . . . an invitation as practical and appealing to business friends as to neighbors, and a style of entertainment that offers great flexibility.

THE COCKTAIL BAR

If you can afford help, a bartender is your best investment. If you can't hire one, accept an offer of help from a friend—for up to twenty-four guests. Above this accept two offers. To find a bartender, if you don't know one by recommendation, call a local college placement service, bartender school, or ask at a nearby hotel. Discuss your plans and prepare your bar setup in advance.

HOW MUCH IS ENOUGH?

If your cocktail party is going to last two hours, allow enough liquor, with extras to offer some choices, to make an average of three drinks per guest. If the party is to last three hours, allow for four to five drinks per guest; if you plan on a cocktail supper, allow an average of a drink and a half per hour per guest—some guests will take only one, while others (physically larger and heavier) may take two or more per hour.

PUNCH-BOWL TACTIC

Some hosts swear by a punch bowl, in addition to individual liquors, as a method of serving a crowd quickly. Choose a liquor with particular appeal to your group, right for the season and the occasion, and a punch bowl can be a blessing in keeping your party moving. If the crowd is too large, and your party will extend for some hours, have the makings ready to refill the bowl quickly.

ORANGE 7 PUNCH

Empty 2 cans (6 ounces each) frozen orange juice concentrate into a punch bowl. Add water as directed for one can. Stir. Add 1 bottle (a fifth, or the 750-milliliter size) Seagram's 7 Crown. Just before serving, add an ice block, 1 large bottle (quart) lemon-lime soda, and 1 cup Leroux Amaretto di Torino. Garnish with orange slices. Makes about 24 punch cups, 4 ounces each.

CRANBERRY VODKA PUNCH

Combine ½ gallon cranberry juice cocktail, 1 bottle (the fifth or 750-milliliter sizes) Wolfschmidt Vodka, in large punch bowl. Set a block of ice or mold in the center. Add 1 quart ginger ale, 1 quart club soda, and stir gently to blend. Garnish with pineapple chunks. Makes about 5 quarts or 40 (4-ounce) servings.

Low-Calorie Punch: Use low-calorie cranberry juice and low-calorie ginger ale, in the recipe above.

CLASSIC EGGNOG

Separate 6 eggs. Beat yolks until pale yellow, beating in ½ cup sugar gradually. Beat egg whites until stiff, but not dry, add another ½ cup sugar. Combine both mixtures. Stir in 1 pint (or 500 milliliters) each heavy cream, milk, and Seagram's 7 Crown. Add ½ cup Myers's Rum. Mix well and serve cold with a sprinkling of nutmeg. Makes about 5 pints or 20 (4-ounce) servings.

EASY EGGNOG

Add 1 cup soft ice cream (can be ice milk) to one quart dairy eggnog. Add 1 pint Seagram's 7 Crown

(500 milliliters), ¼ cup Myers's Rum. Just before serving, shake or beat until frothy. Sprinkle top with nutmeg. Makes about 15 punch cups.

EGGNOG SERVING CHART
Number of Guests

	4-5	10	16	20	40
Seagram's 7 Crown	I cup	I pint	I bottle (4/5 qt.)	I qt.	2 qt.
Eggs	3	6	9	12	24
Sugar	½ cup	I cup	I½ cups	2 cups	4 cups
Cream	I cup	I pint	3 cups	I qt.	2 qt.
Milk	I cup	I pint	3 cups	I qt.	2 qt.
Myers's Rum	I Tbsp.	I oz.	3 Tbsps.	2 oz.	½ cup
Nutmeg	Sprinkling	I tsp.	2 tsp.	2 tsp.	I½ Tbsps.

DELEGATING THE PARTY

One of the great luxuries of party-giving is to turn the party over to someone else—a caterer or a restaurant, hotel, or bar. A cocktail party is more economical for the professionals too and you may find that you can swing such an affair for far less than a dinner situation.

KEEP YOUR IMPRINT

Glasses, ice, napkins—the details of party management are turned over when you plan to have a party catered or at an outside location—but it is still up to you to plan the details of service and menu for foods and drink, to make this a distinctive event. Request the liquors you know you and your friends will enjoy, to give your mark of quality to the event. Find what are the food specialities of the establishment, and take advantage of these in planning your menu.

If the restaurant serves homemade bread, for example, you might simplify your menu with an assortment of cheeses and a cold roast, and baskets of bread and seasoned butters for a do-it-yourself sandwich bar.

ICY POINTERS

Unless you are lucky enough to have an ice maker, stock up on ice cubes in advance of the party. One easy way to do this, if you have a freezer, is to stockpile cubes you make in trays, tumbling them into plastic bags as they are frozen, and storing the bags in your freezer. See Chapter 7 for tips on making very clear cubes.

If you plan on a punch bowl, freeze some larger blocks in bowls, molds, or clean milk cartons. The larger the ice blocks, the slower they melt.

When you go out to buy cubes, the following quick guide may be handy. And if you plan to serve drinks whirled or shaken with crushed ice, it's easier to stock up on a bag of crushed ice—unless you have a bar ice crusher.

NO. GUESTS	2-HOUR PARTY	4-HOUR PARTY	ICE CUBE WEIGHT OR NO.
8	X		5 pounds (about 75 cubes)
8		X	10 pounds
12	X		10 pounds
12		X	20 pounds
24	X		20 pounds
24		X	40 pounds
48	X		40 pounds
48		X	75 pounds

GLASS CHOICES

Even if you own a variety of fine glasses, a large cocktail party without help may be a good time to keep them on the shelf. If you want the tinkle of real glass, rental from a party supply source could be your choice. But the inventor of clear plastic bar glasses deserves a round of applause from the cocktail party planner.

Have two or three glasses available for each guest, for each two hours of party. If you are using disposable glasses, have baskets or bags on hand to collect the used ones as the party progresses. (If you plan to wash these thriftily later, provide a separate container, labeled for glasses only.) A liquor carton with dividers to hold bottles is a handy choice to store stacks of clean plastic glasses, ready for use.

COCKTAIL PARTY STYLES

Partly because this is an idea of our time, the styles of cocktail party service and food offer a broad range of choices. Whether you choose some bowls of eat-out-of-hand nibbles with no service, a complete cocktail supper, or anything in between, add your own "flavor" in food selections, contrasts of tastes, textures, and unexpected favorites to give the party your mark.

1. HELP-YOURSELF NIBBLES

Set out bowls of seasoned popcorn, your own mix-match combinations of nuts, apple sections, and cheese cubes for nibbling, olives tossed with roasted peppers, pretzels of varied sizes combined in a bowl—or oven-heated soft pretzels brought in on a tall dowel set in a flag-holder base. This kind of help-yourself-as-you-like, eat-out-of-hand food is where cocktail parties began.

SPICY "NUTS AND BOLTS" NIBBLE MIX

½ cup butter or margarine
1 tablespoon Worcester-
shire sauce
1 teaspoon chili powder
½ teaspoon garlic salt
½ teaspoon salt
1 cup nutmeats

2 cups bite-size shredded
rice
2 cups bite-size shredded
wheat
2 cups ready-to-eat oat
cereal
2 cups thin pretzel sticks

Melt butter in large baking pan. Stir in Worcestershire sauce, chili powder, garlic salt, and salt. Add nuts, cereals, and pretzels. Stir well. Bake 1 hour in a slow oven (300° F.), stirring every 15 minutes. Store in a tightly covered container; pour into bowls as needed. Makes about 2 quarts.

NUTTY BEANS

Drain and rinse 2 cans (about 1 pound) garbanzo chick peas. Toss on shallow baking pan with 2 tablespoons oil. Bake in 250° F. oven until toasted and golden, stirring occasionally, about 1 hour. Season with salt, fresh-ground black pepper, caraway seeds. Cool and serve as you would nuts.

CHEESY POPCORN

Prepare 3 quarts popcorn, or buy a big bag. Melt ½ cup butter or margarine, skim off foam. Off heat, stir in ½ cup grated Parmesan cheese, dash red pepper, ½ tablespoon salt. Toss mixture with popcorn.

Low-calorie Choice: Toss hot popcorn with 1 envelope dry onion soup mix—no butter or oil.

GARLIC OLIVES

Drain ⅛ of liquid from a jar of olives. Replace with 2 peeled garlic cloves and fill jar with olive oil. Let stand a day or so for garlicky flavor to develop.

CHEESE PASTRY BARS

Place 2 cups flour in a broad bowl. Form a well in the center and cut into this ¼ lb. (½ cup) butter or margarine, softened and cut into pieces, and ½ pound grated Cheddar cheese, ½ beaten egg, 2 tablespoons Seagram's Extra Dry Gin, ½ teaspoon dry mustard. With fork or fingers, beat butter, cheese, liquids, and mustard together, gradually working flour into mixture to form a pastry. Shape into ball. Wrap in waxed paper or foil, and chill. Roll ¼ inch thick on floured board or cloth. Cut into shapes or diagonal bars about ¾ inch by 2 inches. Brush top with remaining egg and sprinkle with poppy seeds, chopped nuts, or sesame seeds. Bake in hot (425° F.) oven about 8 minutes, until golden. Makes about 60 bars.

BOURBON CHEESE BUTTER

Combine ½ pound or 1 pound each of butter and grated sharp cheese, Worcestershire sauce, and 3 tablespoons Benchmark Sour Mash Premium Bourbon per cup of mixture. Whip smooth, and pack into bowl or crock. You can replenish this one with added cheeses, butter, and liquid, to make an everlasting butter. Use as a spread for crackers.

SHRIMP CHIPS

Buy a package of dry shrimp chips in specialty food department or Oriental stores. Drop these by the handful into very hot fat, and watch them billow and puff in minutes. A box makes several big bowls in white or colorful mixture.

BROILED POTATO SLICES

Peel long russet potatoes and cut into very thin slices (¼ inch or less). Brush slices with oil, sprinkle with salt, pepper, paprika, onion salt. Broil on rack 3 inches from heat 4 to 5 minutes each side. Drain and serve hot.

QUICK CURRY DIP

Combine ¼ cup mayonnaise, ½ cup yogurt or sour cream, 1 tablespoon curry powder. Use as dip for broiled potato slices or raw vegetables.

EGGPLANT CAVIAR

Trim ends from 2 large eggplants, bake on flat sheet in hot oven, 425° F., turning occasionally until tender, about 30 minutes. (A microwave oven is excellent for this; reduce baking to about 10 minutes.) Remove, cool slightly, cut open and scoop out the meat. Chop coarsely together with 1 small onion, 1 tomato, skinned and seeded, ½ cup parsley, 4 tablespoons olive oil, juice of 1 lemon, salt, pepper, and paprika to taste. Chill and serve in bowls with buttered thin black bread slices or hot broiled potatoes.

SAUSAGE BITES

Combine 1 pound hot sausage meat or shredded salami with 2 cups grated sharp Cheddar cheese and 3 cups prepared biscuit mix. Roll into balls the size of a marble. Place on baking sheet and bake at 350° F. for 15 to 20 minutes, until golden brown on bottom. Set these out on a wooden tray, for easy self-service.

PORCUPINE

Cut a very thin slice from the bottom of a grapefruit, cantaloupe, or other fresh fruit in season, so that it will stand level on a small board. Use as base to stick all over with cubes of cheese, stuffed olives, radishes, pickles, and other small foods that can be secured on picks.

HOT PORCUPINE

To serve hot nibbles as above, cut a thin slice from an eggplant or cabbage so it will stay level, scoop out center, and imbed a can of Sterno. With picks, stick small sausages, meatballs, marinated broiled meat cubes, and other hot foods all over outside of the vegetable base. Pass the nibbles over flame to crisp.

COLD KEBABS

Alternate colorful, tempting cold items on skewers to please a variety of tastes. Choose from olives, cucumbers, cheese, apple wedges, cherry tomatoes, or an assortment of cold meats. Arrange on trays, garnished with black olives, or serve along with hot, broiled kebabs for interesting contrast.

2. TRAYS OF COLD HORS D'OEUVRE

Whether you make them or buy them, trays of cold hors d'oeuvre are simple to pass, and can be fun fare. You'll find an array of cold hors d'oeuvre choices in the next chapter—but don't stop there. If your time is more limited than your imagination, take your choice of the inventive international treats you can order from restaurants or delicatessens as take-outs.

Or pass trays of do-it-yourself fixings—thin slices of smoked and roasted meats, fish, cheeses, thin-sliced buttered breads, and sliced olives and radishes for toppings—on-the-spot hors d'oeuvre that guests can assemble with one hand, with the other holding a cocktail.

3. FOOL-THE-EYE HORS D'OEUVRE

Add an unexpected note to hors d'oeuvre to liven up the party. A "runner" in the cocktail party circuit is a round of French loaf *en surprise:* The top is cut off, the middle hollowed out and sliced to make small finger sandwiches filled with deviled ham, watercress, and butter, or other simple spreads. These sandwiches are then piled back into the loaf, the top replaced, and the whole tied with a ribbon.

MOCK MUSHROOMS

Skin ½ pound liverwurst and mash. Blend with ½ pound cream cheese, 2 tablespoons Worcestershire sauce, 2 tablespoons Benchmark Sour Mash Premium Bourbon. Chill until stiff enough to mold. Scoop up with tablespoon, roll into ball. Flatten the ball slightly. Press the center with your thumb, in a circular motion, to shape mushroom caps. Reserve a small part of the mixture, roll into a pencil shape, cut off pieces to make stem, attach 1 to each cap. Arrange on rounds of toast, stem side up. Makes about 16.

MOCK CHICKEN LEGS

It looks like a bone, but there never was a chicken young and plump enough to make such rounded little drumsticks! Shape twice-ground chopped meat, seasoned as for meat balls, into the shape of little drumsticks. Roll in mustard-seasoned crumbs and bake about 5 minutes. Pierce with a frilled pick to look like a bone, an easy-to-handle hors d'oeuvre.

No wonder the French have a phrase for hors d'oeuvre—*amuse-gueule*. These will amuse party tasters!

4. TWO GREAT DISHES MAKE A PARTY

If you'd rather make a few hearty dishes than platters of small bites, and you know your party may be dinner for some, two great dishes, one cold and one hot, can do the trick. These might be as simple as a great ham, pre-sliced and glazed . . . or a stuffed breast of veal to slice cold, and turkey scallopini made as you would veal.

STUFFED VEAL

Saute 1 large onion, chopped, in 4 tablespoons oil and 2 tablespoons butter, along with ½ pound chicken livers, until livers are browned but still pink in the center. Chop finely or puree in food processor. Combine with ½ pound spinach, cooked, drained, and chopped; ½ cup chopped parsley; 4 eggs; 2 cups soft bread crumbs. Season with salt, pepper, nutmeg, basil. Mix well. Stuff into the pocket of a breast of veal or a boned shoulder of veal (about 5 pounds before boning) and fasten with skewers. Place in roasting pan, season with salt, pepper, paprika, baste with ¼ cup Myers's Rum heated with ¼ cup butter. Roast loosely covered with foil 1½ hours at 350° F., then uncover and roast another 45 minutes, basting occasionally, until glazed. Serve hot, garnished with carrots and pearl onions, cooked tender and tossed in a hot skillet with butter and Leroux Apricot Liqueur, to glaze. Or chill and serve with tangy mustard pickles. Makes 12 or more servings.

TURKEY SCALLOPINI

Buy 3 pounds boneless turkey breast and slice thin, as scallopini. Place slices between sheets of waxed paper and pound thinly. Dust with flour seasoned to taste with salt, pepper, and a dash of paprika. Brown on both sides. Remove to shallow casserole, arranging in overlapping slices. Pour ¼ cup Seagram's 7 Crown into pan and cook over moderate heat, stirring in any brown bits. Add 1½ cups chicken broth, 2 tablespoons beef glaze, 3 tablespoons tomato paste. Stir over heat until sauce is smooth. Add 1 cup sautéed mushroom slices. Spoon over turkey slices in casserole. Bake in 350° F. oven about 20 minutes, until hot. Serve with noodles. Makes 10 servings.

5. FONDUE IT

A fondue pot for each 6 guests and the cheese, wine, bread makings are all you need to make fun *and* refreshment for a party. See Fondue directions in the next chapter. Remember that anyone who loses a square of dipping bread in the fondue owes a kiss all around!

6. GLAZED CORNED BEEF SANDWICH BAR

You'll enjoy the results more and save money, too, if you prepare your own glazed corned beef for a sandwich tray, another easy way to feed a cocktail party.

LUCKY 7 GLAZED CORNED BEEF

Place a 6-pound corned beef in a large pot, cover with water. Add ½ cup Seagram's 7 Crown, 1 clove garlic, 2 bay leaves, 4 whole cloves, 4 peppercorns. Bring to a boil. Simmer, covered, 3 to 4 hours until tender. Remove corned beef and place in shallow roasting pan. Trim the top fat, score diagonally in diamond pattern. Prepare glaze by combining ¼ cup orange juice, ¾ cup brown sugar, 2 tablespoons corned beef stock, 1 teaspoon mustard, ¼ cup Seagram's 7 Crown in a saucepan. Cook over low heat, stirring until blended. Pour over corned beef and bake in moderately hot (400° F.) oven for 30 minutes, to glaze. Keep corned beef warm on tray, and slice as needed. Add sliced rye with mustard and cole slaw.

7. CHEESE TASTING

Set out an assortment of cheeses for tasting, including some surprise flavors. To make the most of their flavor, cheeses should be served at room temperature, so remove them from the refrigerator at least an hour in advance. This is especially important for semisoft cheeses, such as Brie. Arrange an assortment—mild and strong, chewy, firm, and semisoft—on wooden boards, and leave plenty of room between for easy cutting. Provide an assortment of breads and crackers—and plenty of knives. Complement the flavors and textures of the cheeses with fruit.

HERBED GERVAISE CHEESE

Make your own inexpensive imitation of the French specialty by beating ½ pound fresh cream cheese with 4 ounces cottage cheese, 1 tablespoon each cream, chopped chives, chopped parsley, 1 teaspoon dried crumbled tarragon, salt to taste. Shape into a round, chill, then coat with 1 tablespoon finely cracked black pepper.

8. AROUND THE WORLD AT YOUR PARTY

Add fun to your party by picking a place—someplace you've been, or want to go, or a guest knows, or just a place whose flavors you enjoy. Plan your menu with Greek, Italian, Portuguese, or what-you-will specialties—add posters, records and toast (chart in Chapter 6).

9. COME FOR COCKTAILS . . . STAY FOR SUPPER

That's the best of all cocktail invitations. It means guests can relax at your party, enjoy their evening meal, and you can serve a meal with less fuss than a formal dinner.

The simplest cocktail supper meal to plan is a buffet. It's generally best to start serving this about 1½ hours after your cocktail party begins.

SPIRIT-GLAZED BIRDS

Buy half as many Rock Cornish hens as you will have guests. Season with salt, pepper, ginger, rub lightly with butter combined with Benchmark Sour Mash Premium Bourbon, and roast at 350° F. until tender, about 50 minutes. Cool and split each in half, lengthwise. This may be done in advance. Reheat on foil-lined roasting pan, basting with the sauce below, about 15 minutes at 350° F.

SWEET AND SOUR RUM SAUCE

For 4 to 6 hens, combine 1 can (about 8 ounces) undrained crushed pineapple, 1 clove garlic, crushed, ¼ cup honey, ¼ cup white vinegar, 1 tablespoon soy sauce, ¼ teaspoon each paprika and cayenne pepper. Bring to boil. Combine 1 tablespoon cornstarch and ½ cup Myers's Rum. Add to hot sauce mixture and cook until thickened, stirring constantly. Cool and strain or whirl in blender for ½ minute. Makes about 1¾ cups. Use to glaze.

SWEDISH MEATBALLS

2 cups fresh rye bread crumbs	Pinch each pepper, nutmeg, allspice
1 cup milk	2 tablespoons butter or margarine
2 pounds ground beef	
2 eggs	2 tablespoons flour
½ cup chopped onion	¾ cup beef broth
1½ teaspoons salt	¾ cup light cream

Soak crumbs in milk. Blend well with meat, eggs, onions, and seasonings. Shape into small balls. Heat butter or margarine in a skillet and brown meat balls; remove from pan. Drain all but 2 tablespoons fat. Stir in flour and cook for 2 minutes. Add broth and cream. Cook, stirring, until gravy is smooth. Return meatballs to pan and simmer for 20 minutes, until done. Serve hot in chafing dish, with noodles side dish if as main course. Makes about 40 appetizer servings or 10 main-course servings.

BEEF KEBABS

Cut 3 pounds beef sirloin into 1-inch cubes. On skewers, arrange beef cubes alternately with mushroom caps, cherry tomatoes, green pepper chunks, and small blanched and peeled white onions. In a deep dish combine 1 cup oil, 1½ cups red wine, ½ cup red wine vinegar, ½ cup The Famous Grouse Scotch, salt, pepper, and garlic to taste. Marinate kebabs in mixture, refrigerated, 4 hours or overnight, turning occasionally. Remove from marinade and drain on paper towels. Reserve marinade for another use. Broil kebabs until done, about 10-12 minutes. Makes 12 servings.

SCOTCH BEEF STEW

2 tablespoons butter or margarine
2 tablespoons oil
3 pounds beef top round, cut into 2-inch cubes
24 small white onions, peeled
8 carrots, cut in chunks
4 tablespoons flour
1 tablespoon tomato paste
1¼ cups beef broth or stock
¾ cup red wine
¼ cup The Famous Grouse Scotch
1 teaspoon salt
1 teaspoon pepper
Bouquet garni (stalk of celery, sprig each of parsley, thyme, tied together)
Chopped parsley

In a large heavy skillet, heat butter or margarine with oil. Over high heat, brown beef cubes a few at a time, transferring them to a bowl. Add onions and carrots to skillet. (Onions are easy to peel without tears if you drop them into boiling water for five minutes first.) Saute a few minutes to glaze. Remove to a bowl. Add to a skillet flour and tomato paste, stirring until well blended. If necessary, add additional tablespoon or two of butter to incorporate all the flour. Add stock, wine, Scotch, salt, pepper, bouquet garni, and the browned beef. Cook very slowly, covered, for 1½ hours. Uncover, remove bouquet garni, add the onions and carrots, taste and adjust seasonings. (This may be done in advance.) Simmer about 30 minutes longer, until vegetables are tender. Serve in a casserole, sprinkled with chopped parsley. Makes 8 servings; can serve 16 at a buffet with other offerings.

BARLEY PILAF WITH MUSHROOMS

4 tablespoons butter or
   margarine
1 large onion, chopped
½ pound mushrooms, sliced

1 red pepper, cut into
   strips
2 cups barley
1 quart hot beef or
   chicken broth

Melt butter or margarine in a 2-quart casserole. Add onion and cook, stirring, until golden. Add mushrooms, cook 3 minutes, stirring constantly. Remove mushrooms, set aside. Add red pepper strips, cook 2 minutes to glaze. Remove pepper strips, add to mushrooms. Add barley to casserole and stir until lightly browned. Add broth, stir well, cover and bake in a moderate oven (350° F.) 1 hour, until barley is tender and broth is absorbed. Add mushrooms and pepper strips and cook to heat through. Makes 8 servings, about ¾ cup each.

10

Great Hors D'Oeuvre

Food and beverages go together—and can set each other off to add interest to a party.

Food adds something else, too—it slows down the rate at which your body absorbs alcohol, so it's especially important to offer a variety of appetizing foods when cocktails are the main event. Foods with high fat and protein content stay with you longest, and have the greatest satiety value. This is why cheese, nuts, and meats are favored hors d'oeuvre with cocktails.

Gear your foods to the occasion. For postgame cocktails, for example, you might want to shape your homemade paté into a football and pipe on a mayonnaise lacing. An *après*-ski party calls for hearty, warming fare, perhaps even a steaming "Bloody Mary" soup in cups; while a *bon voyage* party for a Caribbean-bound friend suggests a more tropical motif, in food as well as décor.

It is better to have more small platters, to bring out freshly as needed, than to put your all into one platter that will be half empty for a large part of the party.

ALWAYS ON TAP

Some of the most favored and most elegant hors d'oeuvre are the easiest and quickest to serve. Arrange your raw vegetables in a basket like a bouquet, ring a jar of caviar with circles of chopped hard-cooked egg and chopped olives. Quickies can be as appealing as the most elaborate specialties.

CAVIAR

The best Beluga Malassol caviar demands careful treatment. To serve properly cold, imbed the original tin or jar in crushed ice. Serve with tiny toast rounds, sweet butter, chopped hard cooked egg, and lemon wedges.

For inexpensive glamor, fill a hollowed-out lemon with lumpfish or salmon caviar, surround on a plate with circles of chopped onion, egg yolk, and egg white. Let guests help themselves to toast rounds and lemon.

For Old World elegance, serve caviar with blinis and sour cream. Accompany with ice-cold Wolfschmidt Vodka.

BLINIS

½ envelope active dry
   yeast
¼ cup tepid water
1¼ cups tepid milk
⅔ cup buckwheat flour
⅓ cup white flour

½ teaspoon salt
3 eggs
1 teaspoon sugar
1 tablespoon melted
   butter or margarine

Dissolve yeast in water. Beat in half the milk and half the flours. Cover and let rise in a warm place 2 hours. Beat in remaining flour and salt. Beat eggs with remaining milk and sugar and add to batter with melted butter. Let rise additional hour, covered. Add more milk if necessary to thin batter to consistency of heavy cream. Spoon batter onto hot greased griddle, using 1 tablespoon per pancake. Turn once to brown both sides. Makes 25.

FOIE GRAS

In whatever form you find it, whole or in a paté or mousse, truffled or untruffled, foie gras or goose liver should be served at room temperature or only slightly chilled, not so cold that the flavor is lost. Arrange on a platter with slices of fresh, buttery brioche. Or garnish on a platter with curly lettuce. Serve with crackers.

SMOKED SALMON

For the center of attraction at a big party, buy a whole side of Scotch salmon (imported or domestic, depending on your budget and the occasion of the party) sliced very thin. Overlap it, like shingles, on a chilled platter and garnish with parsley and lemon slices. Serve with toast and butter or with whipped cream flavored with a little carefully drained prepared horseradish.

PROSCIUTTO AND MELON

The Italian variety of the salty, flavorful aged hams is best known, but be sure to check out varieties like West-phalian, Lachschinken, or even Virginia Smithfield ham. Wrap thin slices around melon strips (honeydew or cantaloupe) sprinkle with lime juice, fasten with picks.

OTHER HANDY APPETIZERS

CURRIED WALNUTS

2 tablespoons oil	1 teaspoon salt
2 cups walnut meats	½ teaspoon curry powder
(or other nuts)	Pinch sugar

Heat the oil in a skillet, add nuts and cook slowly, stirring, until golden and crisp, about 7 minutes. Drain on paper towels. Combine remaining ingredients; sprinkle over nuts and toss to blend. Cool before storing in an airtight jar. Makes 2 cups.

TOASTED ALMONDS

¼ cup butter or margarine   1 tablespoon garlic salt
½ teaspoon Tabasco sauce   4 cups blanched almonds
1 tablespoon Worcester-
  shire sauce

Melt butter, add seasonings, and blend well. Add almonds and stir to coat. Spread on a large cookie sheet and toast in 375° F. oven, 15 to 20 minutes. Stir once or twice during toasting. Drain on paper towels, cool, and store in an airtight jar. Makes 4 cups.

ANTIPASTO

Many "instant appetizers" are great by themselves, but put them together Italian-style and you have a sensational hors d'oeuvre platter that's a feast for the eyes as well. The classic antipasto contains salami, sardines, tuna, anchovies, provolone, and other cheeses, celery, olives, fresh and pickled peppers, marinated artichoke hearts, and eggplant caponata. Let your taste guide.

COLD HORS D'OEUVRE

Canapes

Canapes are the basic finger foods and as universal as the cocktail. In essence, they are simply tiny open-face sandwiches.

Mix-match the following basic ingredients to create your own ideas. Make canapes in a variety of shapes and colors and arrange them in patterns on the platter.

1. Base: bread and toast slices cut into circles, squares, rectangles, triangles, diamonds; assorted crackers; pie or pastry dough baked in tiny tart shapes.

2. Spread: Cream cheese, butter or margarine, or mayonnaise, plain or flavored with any of the following:

Chopped parsley, chives, watercress, or other fresh herbs
Lemon juice
Anchovy paste
Capers, drained and chopped
Curry powder
Mustard, dry or prepared
Horseradish

3. Topping:
Caviar and chopped egg
Sliced ham and cheddar strips
Smoked oysters
Salami and cornichons (tiny pickles)
Shrimp and pimiento
Provolone slices and rolled anchovy
Smoked tongue
Beef slivers and sliced radish
Sardines
Hard-cooked egg slices and watercress
Chopped chicken liver, piped on with a star tube
Chicken, tuna, or egg salad, chopped fine, piped on
Cucumber slice and flaked crabmeat
Lox and fresh dill

PINWHEEL SANDWICHES

Trim crusts from an unsliced loaf of white bread. Slice lengthwise, ¼ inch thick. Flatten slices with a rolling pin. Spread with softened butter or margarine or cream cheese and your choice of filling, such as red caviar, finely chopped shrimp salad with watercress, or thinly sliced ham. Roll up slices, starting at the short end. Wrap rolls and chill for 2 hours. Unwrap and slice into ½-inch wheels.

PUFF SHELLS

1 *cup water*	1 *cup flour*
½ *cup butter or margarine*	4 *eggs*
1 *teaspoon salt*	

Bring water, butter, and salt to a boil in a heavy saucepan. Add flour all at once and stir until mixture forms a ball and leaves the sides of the pan. Remove from heat and beat in eggs one at a time, beating well after each addition until smooth. Drop on a greased baking sheet in mounds the size of a walnut. Bake at 400° F., about 8 to 10 minutes, until dry. Cool. Cut off tops. Fill with desired fillings and replace tops. Makes about 36.

Tuna Caper Filling: Drain 1 can (7 ounces) tuna, flaked, and blend well with 4 tablespoons mayonnaise, 2 tablespoons minced capers. Fills 18 puffs.

Quick Paté Filling: Add 3 tablespoons Benchmark Sour Mash Premium Bourbon to 2 cans (4½ ounces each) liver paté. Beat smooth. Fills 18 puffs.

Olive Filling: Whirl ½ pound diced cooked ham, ¼ cup mayonnaise, ¼ cup stuffed olives, and one tablespoon minced onion in a blender. Fills 18 puffs.

Cream Cheese and Lox Filling: Blend 1 package (8 ounces) softened cream cheese with 3 ounces minced lox, and 1 tablespoon chopped chives, 1 tablespoon The Famous Grouse Scotch. Fills 18 puffs.

Shrimp Filling: Blend 3 ounces softened cream cheese, 2 tablespoons sour cream, 1 tablespoon chili sauce, 1 teaspoon horseradish, ½ teaspoon salt. Fold in ½ cup minced cooked or canned shrimp, 2 tablespoons minced celery. Fills 18 puffs.

STUFFED EGGS

Cut 12 hard cooked eggs in half lengthwise, remove yolks, and mash. Blend yolks with your choice of the following ingredients, mound filling in whites, and garnish, as indicated:

- ½ cup softened butter or margarine, 6 tablespoons prepared mustard, ½ teaspoon salt. Garnish with pimiento strips or chopped parsley.

- 1 cup crumbled blue cheese, ½ cup softened butter or margarine, dash Worcestershire sauce. Sprinkle with paprika.

- ¼ cup finely chopped gherkins, 1 teaspoon black pepper, 2 teaspoons salt, 1 teaspoon curry powder, ½ cup mayonnaise. Garnish with chopped parsley.

- ¼ cup sour cream, 2 tablespoons lemon juice. Spoon caviar over filled eggs.

- ¼ cup each butter or margarine and liver paté, 2 teaspoons lemon juice, 1 teaspoon salt. Garnish with sliced green olives.

- 6 tablespoons butter or margarine, 4 tablespoons mayonnaise, 2 teaspoons Worcestershire sauce, 2 teaspoons lemon juice, salt, pepper, and cayenne to taste. Garnish with thin strips of ham.

- ½ cup mayonnaise, ¼ cup deviled ham, 1 teaspoon each of dry mustard, salt, and pepper. Garnish with chopped parsley.

LIPTAUER CHEESE CROCK

1 pound cottage cheese
¼ pound butter, softened
6 anchovy fillets, drained and mashed
1 tablespoon paprika

2 tablespoons each caraway, chopped capers, chopped chives
2 teaspoons prepared mustard

Sieve the cottage cheese and gradually beat into softened butter until smooth. Blend in remaining ingredients. Pack into a crock or mold and chill well. Serve in crock or turn out onto a plate and garnish with pretzels and slices of pumpernickel. Makes 2½ cups.

BOURBON BLUE CHEESE BALL

½ pound blue cheese
½ pound cream cheese
1 tablespoon Bench-
  mark Sour Mash
  Premium Bourbon

1-2 teaspoons Worcester-
  shire
½ cup coarsely chopped
  walnuts

Soften cheeses and blend together well with Bourbon and Worcestershire. Form into a ball and roll in nuts, pressing in firmly. Serve with crackers.

QUICK LIVER PATE

2 tablespoons butter or
  margarine
1 pound chicken livers,
  cleaned
1 cup soft butter or
  margarine
½ small onion, sliced
2 cloves garlic, minced

½ teaspoon each nutmeg,
  dry mustard,
  white pepper
1½ teaspoons salt
¼ cup Benchmark Sour
  Mash Premium Bourbon
1 bay leaf

Heat 2 tablespoons butter in a skillet and cook livers about 4 minutes, until just pink in centers. Add livers to a blender jar with butter, onion, garlic, spices and salt. Pour Benchmark Sour Mash Premium Bourbon into skillet and cook, stirring in any brown bits that cling to the pan. Pour into blender jar. Whirl until smooth and pour into a 4-cup crock or mold. Place bay leaf on top and cover. Refrigerate until set. Makes 3 cups.

SAVORY TOAST STICKS

Trim crusts from a 1-pound loaf of white bread. Slice lengthwise into ½-inch slices, cut slices into strips ½ inch wide and 4 inches long. Roll in melted butter or margarine. Coat ⅓ of the strips with grated Parmesan cheese, ⅓ with dried crushed oregano. Decorate remaining strips with an anchovy fillet. Bake on a cookie sheet at 375° F. for 15 to 20 minutes, until crisp and golden. Cool and store in covered tin or wrap in foil and freeze. Makes about 120 sticks.

BLUE CHEESE DIP

Soften 1 pound blue cheese and blend with ¼ cup heavy cream. Stir in 1 cup chopped walnuts. Makes about 3 cups.

SALMON SURPRISE

3 cans (1 pound each) salmon, drained, skinned, boned
1 package (8 ounces) cream cheese, softened
4 hard-cooked eggs, shelled and chopped

1 medium onion, minced
3 sprigs parsley, chopped
Fine, dry breadcrumbs, if needed
Mayonnaise, if needed

For decoration:

1 or 2 firm, green cucumbers
1 caper
Scallion tips
1 envelope unflavored gelatin

¾ cup cold water
2 tablespoons lemon juice
3 or 4 lemons, thinly sliced
Parsley sprigs

Flake salmon in a large bowl. Add cream cheese, chopped eggs, onion and parsley. Beat until almost smooth, or process quickly in food processor or blender. Do not overblend. Mixture should be stiff enough to hold a shape, but not dry. If necessary, work in breadcrumbs to thicken, or moisten with mayonnaise. Make a cardboard cut-out in the shape of a fish and cover with plastic wrap. Mound mixture onto cut-out and smooth to desired shape. Chill 30 minutes or longer to set. Holding ends of plastic wrap, transfer salmon to a serving platter. Trim off exposed plastic wrap and touch up fish shape. Cut cucumbers in half lengthwise (do not peel) and cut into thin slices. Decorate fish with overlapping rows of slices to form "scales." Use a caper for the eye and the green tips of scallions for tail and fins. Soften gelatin in cold water, heat to dissolve, and add lemon juice. Chill until cool but not set. Brush fish with gelatin mixture to glaze. Decorate platter with thin lemon slices and parsley sprigs. Chill until serving. Makes about 24 servings.

HUMMUS BI TAHINI

1 can (1 pound) chick-peas, drained
¼ cup tahini (sesame seed paste)
1 tablespoon grated onion
1 clove garlic, crushed
1 teaspoon salt
¼ teaspoon pepper
½ cup olive oil
3 tablespoons lemon juice

Purée the chick-peas in a blender or force through a sieve. Mix in tahini, onion, garlic, salt, and pepper. Gradually beat in the olive oil and lemon juice. Refrigerate for several hours before serving. Makes about 2½ cups. Serve with wedges of pita bread as dip.

CHEESE FONDUE

1 pound Swiss cheese, or
   half Swiss and half
   Gruyere, grated
1½ tablespoons cornstarch
1 clove garlic

2 cups dry white wine
¼ teaspoon nutmeg
   Dash white pepper
   Dash Leroux
   Kirschwasser

Toss grated cheese with cornstarch. Heat wine with garlic in a chafing dish over low heat. Remove and discard garlic. Add cheese a handful at a time and stir until melted. Season with nutmeg, pepper, and Kirschwasser. Keep warm over flame. Serve with French bread cubes and long forks for dipping.

SPINACH ROULADE

4 tablespoons butter or
   margarine
¾ cup flour
3 cups milk
1 teaspoon salt
6 eggs, separated

2 packages (10 ounces
   each) fresh spinach,
   trimmed and washed
2 tablespoons butter or
   margarine
½ cup heavy cream
   Salt, pepper, nutmeg

Melt butter in a heavy saucepan. Stir in flour and cook over low heat for one minute. Gradually add milk and salt, stirring until smooth. Simmer for about 5 minutes, stirring, until thick. Remove from heat and beat in egg yolks. Beat egg whites until stiff and fold in. Pour into a 10-by-15-inch jelly-roll pan lined with greased and floured aluminum foil and level with a spatula. Bake at 325° F. for 40 to 45 minutes, until top is golden. Remove and cool slightly. While egg mixture is baking, place washed spinach in a large, heavy pot, cover, and steam in the moisture that clings to the leaves for 2 to 3 minutes, until just wilted. Drain in a colander, pressing firmly to remove excess moisture. Chop. Heat 2 tablespoons butter in a skillet; sauté chopped spinach over medium heat until well coated with butter. Add cream and remaining seasonings. Continue to cook until cream is absorbed and mixture is thick. While roulade is still warm, turn it out onto a sheet of waxed paper and spread with the spinach mixture. Holding waxed-paper corners, roll up lengthwise. Slice roll into rounds ¾ inch thick. Makes 20 servings.

QUICHE LORRAINE AND VARIATIONS

1 9-inch pie shell	1 cup milk
4 strips bacon, cooked crisp and crumbled	1 cup heavy cream
	½ teaspoon salt
1 cup grated Swiss or Gruyere cheese	¼ teaspoon each white pepper and nutmeg
4 eggs, lightly beaten	

Prebake pie shell in 425° F. oven about 8 minutes. Then sprinkle bacon and cheese over bottom. Combine eggs, milk, cream, and seasonings and pour into shell. Bake in a preheated 350° F. oven for 30 to 40 minutes, or until knife inserted near center comes out clean. Cut into 10 or 12 wedges and serve warm.

Variations:

Substitute any of the following for the bacon and cheese:

Crabmeat Quiche: 1½ cups cooked crabmeat, 2 tablespoons each finely chopped onion and celery, 1 tablespoon sherry.

Spinach Quiche: 1 cup cooked, well-drained, chopped spinach, ¼ cup grated Parmesan cheese.

Onion Quiche: 2 medium onions, sliced, sautéed in 2 tablespoons butter or margarine until soft, ¾ cup grated Swiss cheese.

Mushroom Quiche: ½ pound mushrooms, sliced and sautéed with 2 tablespoons butter or margarine and ½ teaspoon lemon juice; 2 tablespoons minced scallions, ½ cup grated Swiss or Gruyere cheese.

SCAMPI

24 jumbo shrimp	1 teaspoon salt
2 cloves garlic, minced	2 tablespoons lemon juice
1 tablespoon chopped parsley	½ cup each olive oil and melted butter or
1 teaspoon oregano	margarine

Peel and devein shrimp, leaving tails on. Split lengthwise without cutting in half, and arrange in a baking pan, tails up. Combine remaining ingredients and pour over. Bake in a preheated 450° F. oven for 4 minutes and slip under broiler for 2 to 3 minutes more to brown. Makes 24 servings.

CHINESE CHICKEN WINGS

½ cup each soy sauce and honey	1 teaspoon prepared mustard
2 tablespoons Seagram's 7 Crown	¼ teaspoon ground ginger
2 tablespoons lemon juice	2 pounds chicken wings

Combine soy sauce, honey, Seagram's 7 Crown, lemon juice, mustard, and ginger in a large shallow bowl. Cut each wing in two pieces at the joint and add to marinade. Refrigerate overnight. Remove from marinade and broil 5 inches from the heat, turning frequently, until well browned and cooked through. Serve hot or cold. Makes about 28 servings.

DEVILED MEATBALLS

1 pound ground beef
¼ cup pickle relish
½ teaspoon salt
⅛ teaspoon cayenne
2 tablespoons oil

½ cup pickle relish
¼ cup chili sauce
Dash Tabasco sauce
1 clove garlic, crushed
½ cup beef broth

Gently toss beef with pickle relish juice, salt, and cayenne until well blended. Form into tiny meatballs. Heat oil in a skillet and brown meatballs on all sides. Combine remaining ingredients and pour over meatballs. Simmer for 10 minutes, until cooked through. Serve in a chafing dish with picks. Makes about 48 tiny balls.

MASHI WARAK (STUFFED GRAPE LEAVES)

1 small onion, minced
1 clove garlic, minced
1 tablespoon oil
¼ pound raw rice
1 pound ground lamb
   or beef
2 eggs, lightly beaten
1 tablespoon chopped
   parsley
1 teaspoon salt

¼ teaspoon each pepper,
   cumin seeds, fennel
   seeds, and cinnamon
⅛ teaspoon turmeric
1 jar grape leaves
   (about 30 leaves)
2 quarts chicken broth,
   hot
   Juice of one lemon

Sauté onion and garlic in oil until soft. Cool. Soak rice in cold water for 15 minutes; drain. Mix together onion, garlic, rice, meat, eggs, and seasonings. Rinse grape leaves in cold water and pat dry. Spoon a little of the meat mixture onto each leaf and roll up tightly, tucking in ends. Arrange in one layer in a large, flat-bottom pan and weight down with a plate. Add hot broth and lemon juice and place in a 375°F. oven for about 1 hour, until leaves are soft and lamb and rice are cooked. Remove from liquid and serve hot. Makes 30 servings.

ANGELS ON HORSEBACK

24 oysters,
   fresh or frozen
 4 teaspoons lemon juice

Salt, pepper, thyme
12 slices bacon,
   cut in half

Sprinkle oysters with lemon juice and seasonings. Wrap a piece of bacon around each oyster and thread on small skewers or picks. Broil, turning to brown, until bacon is crisp. Makes 24 servings.

RUMAKI

 6 chicken livers
18 canned water chestnuts
 9 bacon strips, cut in half

½ cup soy sauce
Pinch ground ginger

Cut chicken livers into 3 pieces. Wrap liver piece and water chestnut in bacon strip and secure with a pick. Marinate ½ hour or more in soy and ginger. Drain and broil until bacon is crisp. Garnish tops of pies with stuffed olive halves. Makes 18 rumaki.

SAVORY MINI TURNOVERS

1 tablespoon oil
1 tablespoon prepared
   mustard
2 tablespoons Seagram's
   Extra Dry Gin
1 jar (4¾ ounces) stuffed
   olives, drained and
   chopped

1 medium onion, chopped
½ cup walnuts, chopped
2 tubes refrigerator
   biscuits dough
1 egg, beaten

Blend oil, mustard, and gin in a bowl. Stir in olives, onion, and walnuts. With a rolling pin, flatten dough into 4-inch circles. Spoon one tablespoon of filling onto each circle, fold over, and press edges to seal. Brush tops with beaten egg. Bake on a greased baking sheet at 425° F. for 10 minutes, until golden. Makes 20 servings.

SOUFFLE MUSHROOMS

24 large mushrooms
4 tablespoons butter or margarine, melted
¾ cup grated Swiss cheese

½ cup dry bread crumbs
4 eggs, separated
¾ cup milk
Salt, pepper

Wash and trim mushrooms. Remove stems and chop enough to make ¾ cup. Sauté in 1 tablespoon butter for a few minutes, and add to cheese and crumbs in a bowl. Blend in egg yolks, milk, salt, and pepper. Beat egg whites until stiff and fold in. Dip mushroom caps in remaining butter and fill with egg/cheese mixture. Arrange on a baking sheet and bake at 400° F. for 10 to 12 minutes, until puffed and brown. Serve immediately. Makes 24 servings.

RUM AND FRUIT KEBABS

½ cup orange juice
½ cup Myers's Rum
2 teaspoons sugar

Pinch ground ginger
3 cups assorted fresh, canned, or dried fruits

Mix together orange juice, rum, sugar, and ginger in a large bowl. Select fruits such as pineapple chunks, tangerine sections, apple wedges, peach or pear slices, dried figs, apricots, or prunes. Add to bowl and marinate 2 hours or longer. Arrange on skewers and broil 3 to 4 inches from heat, until sizzling and beginning to brown. Makes about 20 appetizers.

PROVINCIAL PIZZA ("PISSALADIERE")

1 package yeast roll mix
¼ cup olive oil
2 cloves garlic, minced
8 onions, thinly sliced
2 tablespoons tomato
   paste
½ teaspoon salt

½ teaspoon pepper
½ teaspoon thyme
1 can anchovy fillets
4 slices Swiss cheese, cut
   into strips
18 stuffed olives, sliced

Prepare roll mix according to package directions, or make a batch of your favorite white bread dough. Let rise once and roll out to fit a 10-by-15-inch pan. Heat oil in skillet, add garlic and onion, and cook until soft. Stir in tomato paste and seasonings. Spread onions over dough, arrange anchovies and cheese strips in lattice pattern, and arrange olive slices in between. Bake at 425° F. for 20 to 30 minutes. Cut into small squares. Makes about 36.

BEURRECKS

1 package (1 pound) phyllo
   or strudel leaves
1 pound melted butter or
   margarine

1 pound feta cheese,
   crumbled
1 pound ricotta cheese
2 eggs, beaten

Remove 3 phyllo leaves from the package at a time and stack up one at a time, brushing each with melted butter. Cut lengthwise into 6 strips, 2 inches wide. Mix together cheeses and eggs and place a spoonful of the mixture at one end of each strip. Fold end over end at a 45-degree angle, enclosing the filling. Continue to fold the triangle, as though you were folding a flag. Tuck the last fold under, brush each triangle with melted butter, and arrange on a baking sheet. Bake at 375° F. for 15 minutes until golden. Cool 5 minutes and serve. Makes about 48 servings.

11

Come to Dinner

Say "come to dinner"—and relax. Your vision of a strikingly set table, of delectable appetizers, flawless main course and accompaniments, and elegant dessert can be exactly what you deliver ... even if your setting is casual and your main course a casserole one-dish meal.

Think of a dinner as a play in three acts—whether it takes place in one room, moves from living room to dining room and back to the living room, or even moves from home to home, as a progressive dinner you plan with neighboring friends.

The starters are the first act—cocktails and hors d'oeuvre to open the party.

A preportioned main dish avoids carving at the table, or for a very gracious dinner, a roast that guests will enjoy seeing carved adds drama. For a very large party, a main dish ready to be portioned to satisfy varied appetites is effective. Specifically, this might mean, for a party of six in an apartment, Chicken Breasts Florentine; for a party of eight in a dining-room situation, a Stuffed Crown Roast of Lamb; for a larger buffet-style dinner party, Jambalaya for 12.

This main course is a strong act for your party, and includes accompanying vegetables and distinctive breads.

A distinguished salad rounds off the second act.

For the third act, your dessert is a finale, with coffee or tea before the curtain ... the beverage itself can be part of dessert.

After dinner, your epilogue may be drinks.

Wine poured with main course at dinner adds to the flavor, the texture, and the enjoyment of the meal. The following wine guide lists possible choices for many quality varieties and includes serving tips.

TYPE/REGION	TASTE/SERVING TEMP.	SERVE WITH
FRENCH WINES **B&G** *BORDEAUX—RED:*		
Margaux, Médoc, Prince Noir, St. Emilion, St. Julien, Pontet Latour	Dry, medium-bodied, with delicate, sophisticated fragrance. Serve at room temperature.	Steak, roast beef lamb, cheese.
B&G *BORDEAUX—DRY WHITE:*		
Blace de Blanc, Graves, Pontet Latour, Prince Blanc	Light, dry, slightly soft. Serve chilled.	Grilled, sautéed, or poached fish, oysters.
B&G *BORDEAUX—SWEET WHITE:*		
Sauternes	Rich, sweet, full. Serve chilled.	Pastries, desserts, foie gras.

TYPE/REGION	TASTE/SERVING TEMP.	SERVE WITH
B&G *BURGUNDY—RED:*		
Chassagne-Montrachet; Chateau de Pizay Morgon; Gevrey-Chambertin; Macon Rouge; Nuits-St. George; Pommard	Rich, dry, full-bodied, with a big aroma. Serve at room temperature.	Game, red meats, liver and variety meats, duck, goose, cheese.
St. Louis Beaujolais; Chateau de Pizay Beaujolais Supérieur	Light, dry, fresh, and fruity. Serve lightly chilled or at room temperature.	Roast chicken, turkey, veal, sweetbreads, light stews.
B&G *BURGUNDY—WHITE:*		
Chablis, Macon Blanc, Pouilly-Fuissé, Prince d'Argent, St. Louis Chardonnay	Crisp, dry, light bodied. Serve chilled.	Fish, oysters, cold chicken.
Meursault, Puligny-Montrachet	Dry, full-flavored. Serve chilled but not icy.	Rich fish dishes, lobster, shrimp, chicken.
B&G *RHONE—RED:*		
Chateau-neuf-du-Pape, Domaine de la Meynarde, Prince Rouge	Full bodied, flavorful. Serve at room temperature.	Roasts, stew, highly seasoned meat dishes, cheese.

TYPE/REGION	TASTE/SERVING TEMP.	SERVE WITH
B&G *RHONE—ROSE:* Tavel	Dry, light, refreshing. Serve well chilled.	Chicken, cold buffets, outdoor picnics.
B&G *LOIRE—WHITE:* Muscadet, Pouilly-Fumé, Sancerre, Vouvray	Light, fragrant, fruity. Serve chilled.	Poultry, fish, seafood.
REMY PANNIER *LOIRE—ROSE:* Nectarblanc, Nectarose	Medium dry, delicate. Serve well chilled.	Ham, pork, outdoor picnics.
G.H. MUMM *CHAMPAGNE* Rene Lalou, Cordon Rouge Brut, Cordon Rouge Vintage, Extra Dry	Dry, sparkling. Serve very cold.	Serve alone or with nearly any food.
HEIDSIECK MONOPOLE *CHAMPAGNE* Diamond Bleu Vintage Brut, Brut Vintage Extra Dry		

TYPE/REGION	TASTE/SERVING TEMP.	SERVE WITH
GERMAN WINES JULIUS KAYSER *RHINE—WHITE:* Liebfraumilch Glockenspiel, Bereich Nier- steiner; Black Tower Liebfraumilch	Fruity, rich bou- quet, somewhat sweet. Serve chilled.	Serve alone or with fish, chicken, veal, ham, cheese.
JULIUS KAYSER *MOSELLE—WHITE:* Bereich Bernkastel Riesling, Moselle Bluemchen, Pies- porter Michels- berg Riesling, Zeller Schwarze Katz	Flowery, spicy, light, slightly sweet. Serve chilled.	
ITALIAN WINES BROLIO *RED:* Chianti Classico, Riserva; Ricasoli Chianti	Robust, fragrant, dry. Serve at room tem- perature.	Red meats, pastas.

TYPE/REGION	TASTE/SERVING TEMP.	SERVE WITH
BERSANO Barolo, Barbaresco, Grignolino, Dolcetto Amaro, Barbera d'Asti, Nebbiolo d'Alba	Rich, robust, full-bodied. Serve at room temperature.	
BERSANO Bardolino, Valpolicella	Light, fruity, soft. Serve lightly chilled.	Veal, chicken, light pastas.
LINI LAMBRUSCO Lambrusco	Fruity, somewhat sweet, lightly sparkling.	Alone, or with light luncheons or picnics.
BROLIO *WHITE:* Bianco Bersano Soave	Delicate, dry, light. Serve chilled.	Poultry, seafood, ham.
BERSANO Asti Spumante	Sparkling, somewhat sweet.	Before dinner or with dessert.
AMERICAN WINES PAUL MASSON *CALIFORNIA—RED:* Barbera, Baroque Burgundy, Bur-	Distinguished, flavorful, dry red wines, ranging	All red-meat dishes, stews, game, duck,

TYPE/REGION	TASTE/SERVING TEMP.	SERVE WITH
gundy, Cabernet Sauvignon, Gamay Beaujolais, Petite Sirah, Pinot Noir, Rubion Claret, Ruby Cabernet, Zinfandel	from light and fruity to full-bodied and hearty. Serve at room temperature.	goose, cheese, and spicier veal and poultry dishes.

PAUL MASSON
CALIFORNIA—WHITE:

Chablis, Chenin Blanc, Dry Sauterne, Emerald Dry, French Colombard, Pinot Blanc, Pinot Chardonnay, Rhine, Rhine Castle, Riesling, Johannesberg Riesling	Fresh, dry white wines with delightful aroma. Serve chilled.	All fish dishes, poultry, light meats, light cheese dishes, and casseroles.

PINNACLES SELECTION

Pinot Chardonnay Vintage, Gewurtztraminer Vintage, Johannesberg Riesling Vintage	Full-bodied white wines of great character. Serve chilled.	Chicken, seafood, light meats.

TYPE/REGION	TASTE/SERVING TEMP.	SERVE WITH
PAUL MASSON *CALIFORNIA—ROSE:* Rosé, Gamay Rosé, Vin Rosé Sec	Light, fruity, delicate. Serve well chilled.	Chicken, turkey, salmon, ham, omelettes.
PAUL MASSON *CALIFORNIA— CHAMPAGNES AND SPARKLING WINES:* Champagnes: Brut, Extra Dry, Pink	Light, dry, distinctive. Serve well chilled.	Alone or with any food. On a festive occasion or to make any occasion festive.
SPARKLING WINES: Crackling Chablis, Crackling Rosé, Sparkling Burgundy, Very Cold Duck	Fruity and refreshing. Serve well chilled.	
PAUL MASSON *CALIFORNIA— SANGRIA:* California Sangria	Festive and fruity. Serve chilled, with ice if desired.	Spanish foods, all party fare, or as a refreshing thirst quencher.
PAUL MASSON *CALIFORNIA—VERMOUTH:* Double Dry Vermouth, Sweet Vermouth	Serve on the rocks as an aperitif, or mix them to make martinis, Manhattans, and other cocktails. See Chapter 7.	

TYPE/REGION	TASTE/SERVING TEMP.	SERVE WITH
PAUL MASSON *CALIFORNIA— APERITIF AND DESSERT WINES:*		
Sherries: Pale Dry, Cocktail, Medium Dry, Rare Dry, Rare Flor	Their tangy, nut-like flavor make them famous as aperitifs.	Serve chilled before dinner, with salted almonds, canapes, smoked salmon, other appetizers.
Sweet Sherries: Golden Cream, Rare Cream; Ports: Tawny, Rich Ruby, Rare Tawny, Rare Souzao Muscatel; Madeira	Rich and sweet.	Serve alone after dinner or with dessert or walnuts. Serve Paul Masson Muscatel chilled; Sweet Sherries, Ports, and Madeira at room temperature.
GOLD SEAL *NEW YORK STATE— RED:*		
Burgundy, Burgundy Natural, Catawba Red, Concord, Labrusca;	Red dinner wines with distinctive personalities. American favorites. Serve at room temperature.	Steaks, roasts, ham, chops, cheese and egg dishes, spaghetti, game, heartier foods.
HENRI MARCHANT Lambrusca Red, Catawba Red, Concord		

TYPE/REGION	TASTE/SERVING TEMP.	SERVE WITH
GOLD SEAL *NEW YORK STATE—* *WHITE:* Chablis Nature, Rhine, Chablis, White Burgundy, Sauterne, Catawba White, Pinot Chardonnay Varietal, Johannisberg Riesling Varietal;	Refreshing white dinner wines, from crisp and dry to soft and round in flavor. Serve chilled.	Fish, chicken, all lighter foods.
HENRI MARCHANT Lambrusca White, Catawba White		
GOLD SEAL *NEW YORK STATE—* *ROSE:* Vin Rosé, Chablis Rosé, Catawba Pink;	Fresh light taste that makes them ideal all-occasion wines. Serve well chilled.	Poultry, ham, pork, buffets, and picnics.
HENRI MARCHANT Catawba Pink		

TYPE/REGION	TASTE/SERVING TEMP.	SERVE WITH
GOLD SEAL *NEW YORK STATE— CHAMPAGNES AND SPARKLING WINES:* Brut, Extra Dry, Pink, Sparkling Burgundy, Cold Duck, Blanc de Blancs	Brisk, lively, and effervescent. Serve well chilled.	For all occasions, all meals.
HENRI MARCHANT Brut, Extra Dry, Pink, Sparkling Burgundy, Cold Duck		
GOLD SEAL *NEW YORK STATE— APERITIF AND DESSERT WINES:* Sherry, Cocktail Sherry	Dry, nutlike, appetizing flavor. Serve chilled before dinner with hors d'oeuvre.	
Cream Sherry, Madeira, Port, Ruby Port, Tawny Port	Mellow, full-bodied, sweet. Serve at room temperature after dinner or with dessert.	

EIGHT-BOTTLE BAR: PITCHER OF PERFECT MANHATTANS

In a tall, slender pitcher, stir with ice cubes 750 milliliters (about 3 cups) Seagram's 7 Crown. Add 150 milliliters (⅝ cup) Paul Masson Double Dry Vermouth, 100 milliliters (⅜ cup) Paul Masson Sweet Vermouth, about 1 teaspoon bitters. Have cherries and lemon twists handy. Serve over ice cubes in Old-Fashioned glasses, or in cocktail glasses. Garnish with cherry or lemon twist.

Set out a bowl of toasted almonds, and of a dip—Hummus bi Tahini is quick and satisfying (see p. 163). Choose a hot hors d'oeuvre that's easy to pass in the living room —or on small plates as first course at the table. Shrimp Quiche is easy either way.

SHRIMP QUICHE

1 baked 8-inch pie shell	½ cup milk
1 can (about 4½ ounces) shrimp	½ teaspoon salt
	¼ teaspoon white pepper
¾ cup shredded Gruyère or Swiss cheese	¼ teaspoon dill weed, crumbled
2 eggs, slightly beaten	2 tablespoons grated
1 cup heavy cream	Parmesan cheese

Arrange shrimp and then the Gruyère or Swiss cheese evenly in baked pie shell. Combine eggs, cream, milk, salt, pepper, and dill weed. Pour over cheese-shrimp mixture. Sprinkle top with Parmesan cheese. Bake in preheated hot (425° F.) oven for 15 minutes; reduce oven temperature to 350° F. and continue baking for 15 minutes, or until knife inserted in center comes out clean. Serve warm. Makes one appetizer pie, generous servings for 6. (Or save a wedge or two for the next morning's breakfast. The morning after a party is a breakfast bonus.)

Main dish is baked chicken cooked in the oven with spinach—easy-to-prepare succulent chicken and vegetable in one pan. This provides 2 additional servings for choice—don't be surprised if they all get eaten.

BAKED CHICKEN FLORENTINE

2 broiler fryers, cut up
2 tablespoons melted
 butter or margarine
 Salt, pepper
2 tablespoons dry white
 wine (optional)
3 packages frozen chopped
 spinach

1 medium onion, chopped
1 clove garlic, crushed
 Nutmeg
1 cup sour cream
⅓ cup Parmesan cheese

Lay pieces of chicken side by side in a baking dish. Brush with 1 tablespoon butter and sprinkle with salt, pepper and wine. Pour wine or water into dish. Bake uncovered in a moderate oven (350° F) for 45 minutes, until chicken pieces brown. Meanwhile, steam and drain frozen spinach, and place in bowl. Heat remaining butter in a small pan and cook onion and garlic until soft. Add to spinach and season with salt, pepper and nutmeg. Stir sour cream into spinach mixture. Butter a serving casserole, arrange spinach on bottom, and place chicken pieces on spinach. Sprinkle with Parmesan cheese and bake about 15 minutes longer, uncovered, until chicken is tender. Makes 8 servings.

GNOCCHI

3 cups milk
½ cup butter or margarine
1 teaspoon salt
¾ cup farina

¾ cup grated Parmesan
cheese
2 eggs, beaten

Heat milk, ¼ cup butter, and salt just to boiling. Gradually stir in farina and cook, stirring, until thick. Beat in ½ cup of the cheese; beat in eggs. Turn into a moistened 9-inch square pan, chill until firm. Cut into small squares. Arrange overlapping squares in a greased shallow baking dish or casserole. Dot with remaining butter and sprinkle with remaining cheese. Bake in a moderate oven (350° F.) until golden brown, about 35 minutes. Makes 6 servings.

SALAD EASE

You want a crisp salad to set this off. Cut endive into slices or spears, garnish with pimiento strips, oil, and vinegar dressing—simple to prepare ahead, and the endive will stay crisp.

FOR DESSERT, PETITS POTS AU CHOCOLAT

Almost everyone loves chocolate for dessert, and this is easy to prepare. For extra flavor and texture, put a fresh berry or some peach slices in the bottom of each serving cup, pour chocolate mixture over.

½ pound semisweet
chocolate pieces
1 cup light cream, scalded
4 egg yolks

Dash salt
1 teaspoon vanilla
2 tablespoons Myers's Rum

You can make this quickly in a blender or food processor, or beat rapidly. Put chocolate pieces in container.

Pour scalding hot cream over. Cover, blend 5 seconds, or beat until melted. Continuing to beat, add egg yolks, salt, vanilla, and Myers's Rum. Blend just to combine. Pour into small cups or sherbet dishes. Chill 4 hours or more. Makes 6 servings.

COFFEE FINALE

Serve coffee at the table or in the living room, and offer a choice of dark-roast or decaffeinated—or prepare a specialty coffee drink (see Chapter 15) and make that your after-dinner drink, too.

DINNER FOR EIGHT—SIT-DOWN

In a larger dining room, with more space to set out and show off food, you might plan on a main dish that is carved at the table—as easy as it is dramatic.

Before dinner, set out crisp, colorful crudités for guests to enjoy with their cocktails. For an added savory refreshment, Filled Appetizer Puffs (see p. 159) are easy to make ahead and present on an attractive tray.

Start your dinner with Spinach Velvet Soup, served hot in cool weather, cold during the summer.

SPINACH VELVET SOUP

4 tablespoons butter or
 margarine
1 small onion, coarsely
 chopped
2 tablespoons flour

4 cups chicken broth
3 cups uncooked spinach,
 fresh or frozen
2 cups milk, or half milk
 and half light cream

In a saucepan, heat butter and cook onion until soft. Stir in flour and cook one minute more. Add broth and spinach and stir well. In two or three batches, transfer mixture to a blender container and blend until smooth. Return to saucepan, add milk and cream and seasonings. Bring to a simmer over low heat, stirring constantly. Serve immediately or chill and serve cold.

(NOTE: Soup may require additional salt after it has been chilled. Taste to make sure.) Makes 8 to 10 servings.

STUFFED CROWN ROAST OF LAMB

Crown roast of lamb (16 ribs tied in a circle)
2 teaspoons salt
½ teaspoon pepper
6 tablespoons Seagram's 7-Crown

1 teaspoon dried rosemary
1 teaspoon dried mint
Mushroom Herb Soufflé Filling (see below)

Have the butcher trim the meat from the ends of the rib bones and grind it for you. Season the ground meat with 1 teaspoon salt, ¼ teaspoon pepper, and 2 tablespoons Seagram's 7 Crown, and reserve. Combine 1 teaspoon salt, rosemary, mint, and ¼ teaspoon pepper, and rub into roast. Fold a long strip of aluminum foil in three, lengthwise, and grease lightly. Wrap around the outside of the rib bones to make a collar rising 2 inches above the rib ends, to protect the bones from burning and to hold in the soufflé filling. Place roast in a shallow roasting pan and roast at 325° F. for 45 minutes. Remove from oven. Spoon seasoned ground lamb trimmings into center. Return roast to oven for 15 minutes to set ground meat. Remove from oven and pour off excess fat. Pour soufflé filling into center and return to oven. Roast 40 minutes longer or until filling is puffed and set. Place roast on serving platter and remove foil collar. Surround with Vegetables Bouquetière. To serve, cut between rib bones to separate into individual chops. Serve two ribs per portion, along with some of the soufflé filling. Makes 8 servings.

MUSHROOM HERB SOUFFLE FILLING

¼ cup sliced mushrooms
2 tablespoons butter or
  margarine
1½ tablespoons flour
½ cup hot milk
2 eggs, separated

¼ cup grated Parmesan
  cheese
¼ teaspoon salt
  Pinch each marjoram,
  rosemary, and thyme

In a saucepan over high heat, sauté mushrooms in butter for 1 minute. Reduce heat, stir in flour, and cook 1 minute more. Stir in hot milk and simmer until thickened. Remove from heat; beat in egg yolks, cheese, salt, herbs. Beat egg whites until stiff and fold in.

Nothing sets off a great roast like a Bouquetiére of colorful, fresh vegetables, cooked until crisp-tender and simply dressed with butter and a sprinkle of herbs.

WHEAT PILAF

5 tablespoons butter or oil
1 medium onion, diced
2 cups bulgur wheat

4 cups boiling broth, or
  boiling water plus 5
  bouillon cubes

Heat butter or oil in a large, heavy saucepan, and brown onion lightly. Add bulgur and stir until grains are well coated with fat. Add broth or water and bouillon cubes and bring to a boil. Stir, cover, and simmer over low heat until all liquid is absorbed and bulgur is tender, about 30 minutes. Makes 8 to 10 servings.

VEGETABLES BOUQUETIERE

8–12 small white onions,
    peeled
  4 carrots, peeled and
    cut into 1-inch pieces
  ½ pound green beans,
    trimmed and cut into
    3-inch pieces
  1 small cauliflower,
    separated into
    flowerets

2 ribs celery, cut
  diagonally into 1-
  inch pieces
4 tablespoons butter or
  margarine
  Salt, pepper
2 tablespoons chopped
  parsley

Cook vegetables separately in boiling salted water until done. Heat 1 tablespoon butter in a skillet and sauté onions lightly, until coated with butter. Season with salt and pepper and sprinkle with a little parsley. Continue with remaining vegetables, still keeping them separate and adding more butter as needed. Arrange vegetables in little bouquets around stuffed Crown Roast of Lamb. Makes 8 servings.

APRICOT CLOUD PIE

1½ cups dried apricots
½ cup water
¼ cup Benchmark Sour
  Mash Premium Bourbon
1 envelope unflavored
  gelatin
⅔ cup sugar
1 teaspoon grated orange
  rind

4 eggs, separated
¼ teaspoon salt
1 cup heavy cream,
  whipped
1¼ cups graham cracker
  crumbs
¼ cup melted butter or
  margarine
2 tablespoons sugar

Simmer apricots with water and Benchmark Sour Mash Premium Bourbon over low heat for 10 minutes. Cool slightly. Whirl, with liquid, in a blender or push through a sieve to purée. Mix gelatin well with sugar and add to purée. Stir in orange rind and egg yolks. Cook over low heat, stirring constantly, just until mixture starts to bubble. Chill until it begins to set. Beat egg whites until foamy, add salt, and beat stiff. Stir about ¼ of the whites into apricot mixture. Gently fold in remainder of whites and then the whipped cream. Mix well the graham cracker crumbs, butter, and sugar, and press into a 9-inch pie pan. Spoon in apricot mixture and chill until set. Makes 8 servings.

DINNER FOR TWELVE—
MODIFIED BUFFET

When the crowd is slightly larger, a modified buffet makes serving easy, yet provides a comfortable dining situation. When guests come in to dinner, have three tables for four or one large table set up with silver, centerpiece, or candles, and salads in place. Set out the main course and accompaniments for guests to help themselves. Then serve dessert at the table, and your meal is as graceful as it is convenient.

During before-dinner cocktails, let guests choose hors d'oeuvre from a minibuffet of Deviled Meatballs in a chafing dish, and an Antipasto Tray (see Chapter 10, "Great Hors D'Oeuvre").

Jambalaya, a Creole specialty, is an irresistible invitation to the buffet table.

JAMBALAYA

1 tablespoon oil
1 pound sweet pork
  sausage, sliced
1 pound hot pork sausage,
  sliced
1 pound ham, cut into
  ½-inch cubes
1 green pepper, seeded
  and diced

1 large onion, sliced
1 clove garlic, minced
2 cups raw long-grain rice
1 can (1 pound, 14 ounces)
  tomatoes
2 cups chicken broth
  Salt, thyme, cayenne

Heat oil in a large skillet and add sausage, ham, green pepper, onion, and garlic. Cook, stirring, until meat browns. Stir in rice and cook until light golden. Add tomatoes, broth, and seasonings. Cover, bring to a boil, and simmer 15 minutes, until rice is tender. Serves 12.

With a tossed salad of mixed greens, pass a bowl of oil and vinegar or Blue Cheese Dressing, quickly made by beating together 4 ounces (about 1 cup) crumbled blue cheese, 1 cup mayonnaise, 1 cup sour cream, and 2 tablespoons wine vinegar. Or offer a choice of dressings, and make one of them tangy Green Goddess.

GREEN GODDESS DRESSING

1 cup mayonnaise	¼ cup fresh chopped
½ cup sour cream	parsley
¼ teaspoon garlic powder	¼ teaspoon black pepper
2 green onions, with tops	3 anchovy fillets
2 tablespoons lemon juice	

Whirl all ingredients in a blender until smooth. Makes about 2 cups.

For dessert, continue the "serve yourself" theme and pass a tray of elegant fruit tarts at the table.

FRUIT PASTRY TRAY

For Tart Shells:

2 cups flour	1 cup butter or margarine,
2 tablespoons sugar	softened
Pinch salt	2 tablespoons cold water
2 egg yolks	1 teaspoon lemon rind

Sift flour, sugar, and salt into a mixing bowl. Make a well in the middle and add the remaining ingredients. Gradually work in the flour to make a dough. If necessary, add a few drops of cold water to moisten the dough enough so that it can be gathered into a ball. Wrap and chill one hour. Divide dough into 12 equal pieces. Pat pieces into individual 2½-inch tart shells to cover sides and bottoms. Prick with a fork. Put shells on a baking sheet and bake in a 450° F. oven about 10 minutes. Cool.

For Filling:
⅔ cup sugar
6 egg yolks
4 tablespoons cornstarch
2 cups milk
1 tablespoon butter

¼ cup Myers's Rum
½ cup heavy cream,
* whipped*

Beat together ⅓ cup sugar, the egg yolks, and cornstarch until smooth. Combine remaining ⅓ cup sugar with the milk in a heavy saucepan and bring to a boil. Add the hot milk to the egg mixture in a thin stream, beating constantly. Return the mixture to the saucepan and bring to a simmer. Cook over low heat, stirring, for a few moments, until custard is thick. Remove from heat and beat in butter and rum. Chill thoroughly. Fold in whipped cream. Fill the bottom of each tart shell with about 3 to 4 tablespoons of the chilled filling.

For Fruit Topping:
Use your choice of fresh berries, seedless grapes, sliced bananas, well-drained poached or canned peach halves, apricots, plums, or pears, or pineapple pieces. Arrange on filled tart shells to cover cream filling.

For Apricot Glaze:
Heat 1 cup apricot jam until melted; push through a strainer. Add 2 tablespoons Myers's Rum and heat just to a bubble. Let stand until cool but still liquid, and spoon over fruit tarts to glaze. Arrange tarts on a tray.

12

Parties for
a Few of You

Sometimes two are all you want for a party . . . or a foursome of very good friends. Forget the crowds and the large dishes, and concentrate on creating a time and a mood of special quality.

COCKTAILS FOR TWO OR FOUR

Cocktails are easier to plan when you know the tastes of the guests. Now your challenge is to make the way you serve, and the quality of what you serve, absolutely flawless. This is the occasion to chill the cocktail glasses, as well as the contents, and have them waiting in the freezer, in frosty perfection.

Add a fresh touch to favorite drinks, too. If martinis are a choice, serve a Midnight Martini, with a black olive; or a zesty note for one who likes sharp tastes—a small hot chili pepper in the drink.

If tall drinks are a choice, this is your time to bring out the costly mineral water mixer. When the group is small, Crown Royal can greet a favored guest royally, or The Glenlivet will gladden a Scotch drinker's heart.

INTIMATE HORS D'OEUVRE

Let's face it: You wouldn't want to make a molded paté, or a large-size quiche, just for the two of you, or even for four. But here are a baker's dozen of hors d'oeuvre ideas to welcome one guest or more—and none take more than fifteen minutes to prepare.

1. **Caviar Quail Eggs:** Open a can or jar of quail eggs (sold in Oriental food stores). These are ready-to-eat, hard-cooked, and packed in brine. Drain the liquid, cut the narrow end off the top of each egg, and a tiny slice off the bottom, so it will stand flat. Set on a small lettuce leaf, or arrange flat on a small plate, and top with a dab of caviar or caviar paste from a tube.

2. **Stuffed Cherry Tomatoes:** Cut tops from tomatoes, scoop out, and fill with cheese, or with rolled anchovy.

3. **Hot Artichokes:** Drain an 8-ounce can of artichoke hearts, dry with paper towel. Combine 2 tablespoons Seagram's Extra Dry Gin, ½ teaspoon salt, ¼ teaspoon pepper, dash hot red pepper sauce, 1 teaspoon prepared mustard, ½ teaspoon Italian herbs. Turn the hearts in the mixture, to coat thoroughly. Lift out hearts and drain on saucer. To remaining gin mixture, add an egg, 2 tablespoons cream, and 3 tablespoons flour, beating with a fork. Dip artichoke hearts in batter, spoon out one at a time, turning to cover entirely, then fry in about ½ inch hot oil or butter. Serve with forks and lemon wedge.

4. **Red Peppers and Anchovy:** Open a jar (5 ounces) of roasted red peppers and a can (2 ounces) of anchovy fillets packed in oil. Crisscross two anchovies on a whole pepper. Pass the pepper mill.

5. **Guacamole:** Keep an avocado handy, and when it's ripe and fragrant, invite a friend to dip with you. Cut avocado in half, lengthwise. Remove seed (plant it later) and scoop out the pulp into a shallow soup plate. Mash coarsely with a silver fork—guacamole should not be too smooth. Finely dice a shallot or a green onion; add to avocado along with juice of half a lime; small tomato, peeled, seeded and diced; salt; pepper, dash of taco sauce. Serve with corn chip dippers.

6. **Caponata:** This savory saute of eggplant, diced red peppers, celery, capers, olives, tomatoes, and onions is

ready to serve when you open the small can. Stir with a spoonful of Myers's Rum for extra flavor. Spoon onto crackers or endive leaves, or serve on a small plate.

7. Cheese Puffs: Combine ½ cup sharp cheese, cut in cubes, 1 egg, 1 green onion, a tablespoon of Seagram's 7 Crown in blender container and whirl smooth, or mash and beat thoroughly with a fork. Pile onto 6 to 8 rounds of French bread, spreading to the edges. Broil about 3 minutes, until topping puffs and browns. Serves 3 to 4.

8. Raw Mushrooms: Wipe fresh mushrooms clean and dip into Italian salad dressings.

9. Steak Tartare: Buy ½ pound lean round steak or porterhouse and have this freshly ground for tartare. Season with salt, fresh-ground pepper, chopped onion, 2 tablespoons Benchmark Sour Mash Premium Bourbon. Mound on board, indent center, and drop in 1 egg yolk. Work this into meat along with 2 chopped anchovies, 1 tablespoon chopped parsley. Remound. Serve with lemon wedges, capers, thin-sliced black bread.

10. Smoked Clams or Oysters: Drain and season with a sprinkling of The Famous Grouse Scotch. Serve on cucumber slices or with thin-sliced party rye.

11. Scotch Cheddar: Shred ½ lb. Cheddar, or whatever sharp cheese or combination you have on hand. Moisten with ¼ cup The Famous Grouse, add 1 teaspoon caraway seeds. (If cheese is very cold, heat The Famous Grouse slightly.) Mash well. Pack into a crock.

12. Fondue Bourguignonne: Pick up ½ pound of the finest sirloin or filet, cut into ½ inch cubes. Mound on board with chopped scallions. At the table, season meat with fresh-ground pepper. Heat ⅓ cup oil, ⅓ cup butter in a small pan; skim off foam. Spear cubes of meat on long-handled fork and dip into sizzling fat, holding about 1 minute, to cook. As each cube cooks, slip from hot dipping fork to eating fork, dip into steak sauce combined with The Famous Grouse or mustard cut with Benchmark Sour Mash Premium Bourbon—or both!

13. Zesty Cream Cheese: Place block of cream cheese on a dish, and coat all over with chopped dill or herbs or spices to taste, or cover top with zesty steak sauce.

DINNERS FOR TWO OR FOUR

A small dinner can be a jewel of a party. Bring out your best for the table setting. Light up the candles, and plan on dishes that are perfect for a few guests.

FRESH MUSHROOM SOUP

1½ tablespoons butter
1 teaspoon curry powder
1 shallot or small fresh onion, chopped
1 teaspoon cornstarch
2 cups cold chicken broth

1½ cups mushrooms with stems
1 cup light cream
Salt, pepper
2 mushrooms, thinly sliced

In saucepan, melt butter, add curry and shallot, cook for a few minutes, stirring. Add cornstarch to ½ cup broth, stir into saucepan, and cook until the soup comes to a boil. Wipe mushrooms clean. Cut up and put into blender container with the hot soup, whirl smooth, or purée by hand. Add remaining broth. Add the cream, heat, and simmer a few minutes. Taste and adjust seasoning. Garnish with mushroom slices. Good hot or iced. Makes 3 cups or 4 soup-cup servings.

ROAST ROCK CORNISH HENS WITH RAISIN-RUM RICE STUFFING

4 Rock Cornish Hens,
    about 1 pound each
    Salt, pepper, ginger
1 cup cooked rice
4 tablespoons butter

4 teaspoons minced onion
2 tablespoons raisins
4 teaspoons minced parsley
½ teaspoon nutmeg
⅓ cup Myers's Rum

Dry hens and season with salt, pepper, ginger. Combine rice with 2 tablespoons melted butter and minced onion in skillet. Saute, stirring until golden. Add raisins, parsley, nutmeg, 2 tablespoons rum. Stuff hens with rice mixture and truss. Place stuffed hens breast side up, on a rack in shallow roasting pan; brush with remaining melted butter. Roast uncovered in 375° F. oven for 50 minutes, or until golden and tender, basting with pan drippings and remaining rum. Arrange on serving plate.

HEARTS OF PALM SALAD

1 can (about 14 ounces)
    cut hearts of palm
1 can (8 ounces) pitted
    black olives

3 tablespoons oil
    Salt, pepper, pinch
    mustard
1 tablespoon lemon juice

Drain hearts of palm. Drain black olives and combine with palm in salad bowl. Combine oil, salt, pepper, pinch of mustard, lemon juice. Pour over salad and toss.

RUM CHOCOLATE PARFAITS

1 cup chocolate cookie
    crumbs
2 tablespoons Myers's Rum

1 pint coffee ice cream
    Whipped cream
    Myers's Rum Chocolate
    sauce

Roll or blend cookies to make crumbs. Add rum to crumbs. Spoon a little ice cream into the bottom of each of 4 tall, slender parfait glasses. Top with spoonful of rum-crumb mix. Repeat until you have 3 layers of ice cream, each topped with rum-crumb mix. Finish with whipped cream and Chocolate Sauce: beat 4 ounces semi-sweet chocolate pieces with a jigger of Myers's Rum, stirring until smoothly melted. Makes 4 servings.

COFFEE FINALE

If you serve coffee, make it a distinguished part of the meal. Pass some of the whipped cream used on the dessert, and instead of sugar, use the chocolate rum sauce—a whole new thing in coffee.

After-dinner conversation flows around the table . . . until you start a record for dancing, or a song for two. Offer cordials or highballs after dinner or drinks such as the V.O. Stinger or White Alexander. And make one for the road coffee, or a glass of chilled juice or soda.

HAPPY ENDINGS

The best of parties, particularly a small party, may need a cue from you for a happy ending. You might say, "This is so nice, I hope you will come again," and move toward the door—smiling.

And you'll mean it. The best part of a small party is that you can enjoy all your guests thoroughly!

Whatever your lifestyle, a party can add riches— without excess.

Come for Dessert and...

Your Own Coffee Bar at Home

PART 4

Come for coffee and...

Spirited International Accents

Mocha and Other Favorites

Delectable Desserts

Party Diet

Have Party Will Travel

How to plan a Big Bash

Until the Next...

13

Come for
Dessert and . . .

The best of all parties for you to plan may be one that starts late in the evening . . . after work and a fussless dinner, or after children are asleep, and when your friends really have time to relax and talk. Invite a group for coffee and . . . make the "and" something more than just coffee. Make it a new international blend of coffee (or tea or hot chocolate) and liquor in a range of flavor choices. A "dessert cart" of two or three cakes and pastries makes serving easy and frees you to enjoy the party.

INTERNATIONAL COFFEES MADE EASY

Back of the international array of coffees on the menus of some of the most prestigious coffee houses is one large coffee pot, with a robust dark brew—sometimes a standard coffee combined with espresso roast. Others have large espresso machines for specialty preparations. Whether you prepare your brew in your drip or electric pot, using specialty beans, or in a steam-quick extraction such as espresso, your beverages take on new flavors and warmth with liquor additions, and serving flair.

CANADIAN COFFEE

Brew your favorite coffee. Pour a 1 ounce "pony" of Seagram's V.O. into a goblet for each drink, add a spoon of maple syrup, leave spoon in glass to absorb heat, fill with hot coffee. Top with unsweetened whipped cream.

SLIM CANADIAN COFFEE

Prepare as above, use sugar substitute in place of maple syrup; omit whipped cream.

ESPRESSO ROYALE

Pour espresso into cup, place a round-bowl spoon across the top of the cup. Place small sugar cube in spoon, fill with Benchmark Sour Mash Premium Bourbon, and watch for the sugar to soften. Lower gently into the coffee, and stir.

HOT BROWN COW

3 ounces strong hot coffee
2 ounces Myers's Rum
3 ounces hot milk

Pour milk and coffee into 8-ounce highball glass or mug. Add Myers's Rum, stir, and serve. Sprinkle top with nutmeg if desired.

Fill a coffee decanter, 6 cups size, with freshly brewed coffee, and keep hot. Pour ⅓ cup Seagram's 7 Crown into ladle and hold over the hot coffee. Add 6 cubes of sugar to the liquor, and cubes will soften. Lower the ladle into the decanter and stir gently. Makes 12 demitasse servings.

INTERNATIONAL COFFEE FOR A MOB

1 pound coffee, brewed
1 pint heavy cream
  sugar cubes
1 bottle (1.75 liter) Seagram's 7 Crown, or Benchmark
  Sour Mash Premium Bourbon, or Myers's Rum, or
  Wolfschmidt Vodka—or smaller bottles with a choice
  offered

Prepare coffee in large urn, to make 40 cups—or fewer, if
you want extra-strength coffee. Lightly whip cream. To
serve, guests pop a cube of sugar in a glass, add an ounce
of their favorite liquor, fill ⅔ full of fresh hot coffee, top
with whipped cream, and sip.

CAFE DIABLE

6 ounces Benchmark Sour
  Mash Premium Bourbon
  peel of 1 lemon
8 cloves

1-inch piece cinnamon
  stick
6 teaspoons sugar
4 cups strong hot coffee

Combine Bourbon and remaining ingredients, except
coffee, in top of 6-cup chafing dish, or in decorative
saucepan on a warmer. Stir mixture to warm through and
release flavors, stirring with a long-handled spoon. Slowly add coffee. Ladle into small cups. Makes 8 servings.

CHILLED COFFEES

CAIRO COFFEE—
a coffee cooler good year-round.

4 jiggers Wolfschmidt
  Vodka
1 quart iced coffee
  sweetener to taste

1 pint vanilla ice cream

In a pitcher, stir vodka, coffee, and sweetener with ice. Add a scoop of vanilla ice cream to each of four tall 14-ounce glasses. Pour in coffee mixture. Serve with straws. Makes 4 servings.

COFFEE FRAPPE

2 cups finely crushed ice
2 cups double-strength
    coffee
2 tablespoons sugar
    dash ground cloves
    dash ground nutmeg

4 ounces Benchmark Sour
    Mash Premium Bourbon
    or Myers's Rum
½ pint vanilla ice cream

Divide the ice among 4 slender goblets. Measure the remaining ingredients into blender or shaker, cover and whirl smooth, but do not overmix. Pour the frappé over ice. Serve with straws. Makes 4 servings.

SPIRITED ICED COFFEE

Brew extra-strong coffee, allowing 3 tablespoons coffee for each 6 ounces water (1½ times usual strength). Chill until serving time. Pour over ice cubes in tall glasses, pass decanters of favorite spirits, and a bottle of Leroux Amaretto for sweetening and flavoring. Add whipped cream flavored with Amaretto to crown each glass.

SEVEN-CROWN TEA FLIP

1 jigger Seagram's 7 Crown	small cinnamon stick
1 teaspoon sugar, or to taste	long, thin strip of lemon peel
hot tea	3 cloves

Combine Seagram's 7 Crown, sugar, tea, and cinnamon stick in a glass or china mug. Stud lemon-peel strip with cloves and hang over side of mug. Sip slowly!

BENCHMARK SPICED TEA PUNCH

1 bottle (750 milliliters or about a fifth)
  Benchmark Sour Mash Premium Bourbon
2 quarts freshly brewed hot tea (about 2 liters)
½ teaspoon each cinnamon and ginger
3 tablespoons sugar

Combine Bourbon and tea. Mix cinnamon and ginger with sugar and stir into Bourbon mixture. Ladle hot punch from bowl into small tea cups. Makes about 18 tea-cup servings.

YOUR OWN DESSERT CART

For a dessert cart, provide a few desserts with contrasts of flavor, texture, and color. For example, serve a high and handsome Nesselrode Pie; flavorful, light Babas Au Rum; or Circe's Rum Cake, which follows. Add a bowlful of Rum Balls for extra nibbling, and a bowl of fresh fruit for choice.

Don't be surprised if guests want to taste a little of each —be prepared to cut small portions.

NESSELRODE PIE

2 envelopes unflavored
   gelatin
3 cups milk
6 eggs separated
1 cup chopped glacé fruits
   and peels
¼ cup Myers's Rum
1 tablespoon Leroux
   Apricot Liqueur

Pinch salt
⅔ cup sugar
9-inch graham cracker
   crumb shell
semisweet chocolate
   shavings

Sprinkle gelatin on milk in saucepan, add egg yolks, stir over low heat or in the top of a double boiler over hot water, until gelatin is dissolved and custard coats the spoon, about 15 minutes. Cool. Soak fruit in rum. Add to custard with apricot liqueur and salt. Chill until the mixture begins to set and will mound in a spoon. Beat egg whites foamy, beat in sugar, and continue to beat until stiff. Fold into gelatin mixture and chill until it begins to set. Pile the filling into a graham cracker crumb shell, as high as possible. If necessary, chill filled pie until set, pile on any remaining mixture. Chill several hours, until set. Garnish with chocolate shavings.

BABAS AU RUM

1 envelope active dry yeast
½ cup lukewarm water
¼ cup sugar
1 teaspoon salt

4 eggs, lightly beaten
½ cup butter or margarine,
   melted and cooled
4–5 cups flour

Syrup:
1 cup sugar
½ cup water
½ cup orange juice

1 teaspoon grated orange
   rind
⅔ cup Myers's Rum

Mini-Babas: In mixing bowl, soften yeast in water. Beat in sugar, salt, and eggs. Add melted butter. Gradually add flour, beating with a wooden spoon until dough starts to pull away from sides of bowl. Turn out on lightly floured board and knead until smooth and elastic. Place in oiled bowl, oil top lightly. Cover with a towel and let rise in a warm place until double in bulk, about 1 to 1½ hours. Fill about 3 dozen 3-ounce paper cups ⅓ full, or use empty 6-ounce frozen-juice containers. Cover and let rise until doubled in bulk again. Bake in preheated 425° F. oven 10 minutes; reduce heat to moderate 350° F. oven and bake 20 to 25 minutes more, until brown. Let stand 5 minutes. Turn out on rack.

Syrup: Combine sugar and water in saucepan and bring to boil. Boil for 8 minutes, add orange juice and rind; boil 5 minutes more. Remove from heat. Stir in Myers's Rum. Prick Babas all over with fork and baste with hot syrup until syrup is absorbed. Makes 2 to 3 dozen.

EGGNOG SOUFFLE

2 *envelopes unflavored gelatin*	½ *tablespoon vanilla*
1½ *cups sugar*	⅛ *teaspoon nutmeg*
1½ *cups milk*	12 *egg whites*
8 *egg yolks, lightly beaten*	*pinch salt*
½ *cup Benchmark Sour Mash Premium Bourbon*	2 *cups heavy cream, whipped*
	chopped walnuts

Stir gelatin with ½ cup of the sugar until well combined. Add milk and egg yolks, and using a whisk, beat in a double boiler over simmering water until custard thickens enough to coat the back of a spoon. Add Bourbon, vanilla, nutmeg and cook until mixture thickens again. Chill, stirring often, until mixture just begins to set. Beat the egg whites with salt until thick, beat in remaining sugar, and whip until stiff. Fold into custard. Fold in ¾ of the whipped cream. Lightly butter a band of waxed paper or foil and fasten around the top of a 2-quart soufflé dish to form a collar 2 inches over the top of the dish. Pour in soufflé mixture and chill until firm. Remove collar, decorate with remaining whipped cream. Makes about 20 servings.

CIRCE'S RUM CAKE

½ cup butter or margarine
¼ cup Myers's Rum
1 cup sugar
2 eggs
2 cups flour
3 teaspoons baking powder

¾ teaspoon salt
½ cup milk or cream
1 cup semi-sweet chocolate pieces
½ cup chopped nuts

Frosting:
1 package (12 ounces) semi-sweet chocolate morsels
½ cup (¼ pound) butter
2 tablespoons Myers's Rum

Cream butter with rum and sugar until light. Add eggs one at a time, beating well after each addition. Toss flour, baking powder and salt together; add dry ingredients to creamed mixture alternately with milk or cream. Stir in chocolate pieces and nuts. Spread batter in a greased 8-inch tube pan. Bake in preheated 350° F. oven about 45 minutes. Cool 5 minutes before removing.

For Frosting: Melt together chocolate and butter over very low heat, stirring constantly. Remove from heat, cool slightly and stir in rum. Let cool a few more minutes, until slightly thickened but still pourable. Place cake on rack over a baking sheet. Pour icing over cool cake, letting it run down the sides to cover completely. Decorate with sliced almonds. Let cake stand until icing is set.

RUM BALLS

In a bowl combine 2½ cups crushed vanilla wafer crumbs, ⅓ cup Myers's Rum, ½ cup honey, 1 pound ground pecans, and mix thoroughly. Shape into balls with a round table-spoon measuring spoon. Roll balls in confectioner's sugar. Store in a covered container. Makes 4½ dozen.

Party Diet

You can plan a party without regrets—even for dieters in the crowd. Whether you let guests in on the plot or keep it a secret between yourself and those dieters who care, a party can be fun and good-tasting—and you won't ever have to worry where the calories went.

DIET HORS D'OEUVRE

This means that in hors d'oeuvre, for instance, you might begin with a huge bowl of vegetables for nibbling—and make them interesting: raw asparagus, stems trimmed; pimiento strips, raw mushrooms, sliced radishes, zucchini sticks. Add mustard to yogurt for zesty dipping.

CARPACCIO—*Raw Beef Slices with Green Peppercorns*

1 *pound very lean beef sirloin*
1 *tablespoon green peppercorns, drained*
1 *small clove garlic, peeled*
1 *tablespoon mustard*

1 *teaspoon horseradish pinch each of thyme and basil*
1 *cup Low-Calorie Mayonnaise (recipe follows)*

Trim fat and chill meat in freezer about half an hour to make it easier to slice wafer-thin. Cut across the grain, in thinnest possible diagonal slices. In blender or food processor, or with mortar and pestle, mash green pepper-corns, garlic, mustard, horseradish, thyme, and basil until smooth. Stir this purée into the Low-Calorie Mayonnaise. Arrange a lettuce leaf on each chilled serving plate, top with beef slices, and spoon mustard sauce over meat.

LOW-CALORIE MAYONNAISE

2 cups low-fat cottage
   cheese
¼ cup yogurt
1 egg
2 teaspoons prepared
   mustard

2 tablespoons olive or
   peanut oil
1 small clove garlic, peeled
   Salt and white pepper,
    to taste
   juice of ½ lemon

Combine ingredients in food processor or blender, or beat with a blending fork, at high speed, until mixture is light and smooth. Taste and adjust seasoning. Store in the refrigerator. Makes about 2¼ cups "mayonnaise."

SPICED CHICKEN SPREAD

1 pound chicken breast
2 tablespoons diced
   chicken fat
1 bay leaf
2 cloves
3 garlic cloves, minced

1 small onion
1 tablespoon boiling water
1 ounce Myers's Rum
   pinch each of ground
    cloves, thyme
1 teaspoon salt
1 teaspoon pepper

Cut the chicken meat in one-inch cubes. Cook the diced chicken fat in a range-to-oven casserole over low heat until the fat begins to melt. Add chicken cubes, bay leaf, whole cloves, garlic, onion, water, and rum. Cover the casserole tightly and braise in a moderately slow oven (325° F.) for 1 hour. The chicken will be very soft. Discard bay leaf and cloves. Cool and purée in a food processor or blender. Add ground cloves, thyme, salt and pepper, and combine. Makes about 1 pint.

PICKLED SHRIMP

1½ *pounds raw shrimp*
½ *cup dry white wine*
½ *cup water*
2 *bay leaves*
2 *tablespoons olive oil*
2 *green onions, chopped*
½ *cup fresh lemon juice*
1 *teaspoon tarragon*

dash Tabasco sauce
1 *tablespoon Worcestershire sauce*
½ *teaspoon salt*
dash fresh-ground pepper
2 *tablespoons chopped fresh parsley for garnish*

Peel and devein shrimp, keeping tails intact. In a heavy 10-to-12-inch skillet, cook the shrimp in the wine and water with bay leaves until pink, about 6 minutes. Drain shrimp. Strain stock. In bowl, combine strained stock, oil, onions, lemon juice, and seasonings. Stir well, add shrimp, and toss to coat shrimp thoroughly with marinade. Cover and chill, stirring occasionally. Serve shrimp with some marinade.

FISH PATE

1 pound bass fillet,
   skinned and boned
¼ cup dry white wine
1 shallot, peeled and finely
   minced
1 clove garlic, peeled and
   finely minced
   Pinch each of dry
      tarragon, thyme
1 teaspoon chopped
   parsley

2 large egg whites
¼ cup ricotta cheese
1 cup milk
   salt and pepper
1 teaspoon oil
1 cup Low-Calorie Hollan-
   daise Sauce (recipe
   follows)

Buy a small whole bass, about 3 pounds, and have the
fish man remove half as a fillet. Reserve the other half
to bake for another meal. Put the fillet in a shallow glass
bowl and add wine combined with shallots, garlic, tarragon, thyme, and parsley. Weight the fish down lightly
with a plate and cover the bowl. Marinate 2 to 3 hours.
Drain the fish and reserve the marinade. Cut one fourth
of the fish into thin strips and set aside. Dice the remaining fish in food processor or blender container. Add
the egg whites and blend until smooth. Add the ricotta
cheese and milk and blend to make a smooth pâté. Season with salt and pepper. Lightly coat 4 individual
ramekins or baking cups with oil. Divide half the fish
pâté among the terrines. Arrange reserved fish strips on
top. Cover with remaining pâté mixture. Cover dishes
tightly with aluminum foil and set them in a pan of
hot water. Bake in a hot oven, 400° F., about 15 minutes, just until pâté is set and a skewer inserted near the
center comes out clean and dry. Drain off any liquid that
forms on the surface. Meanwhile, boil the reserved
marinade in a shallow pan over high heat until it is re-
duced to 2 tablespoons. Add Low-Calorie Hollandaise
Sauce, and stir over moderate heat just until hot. To serve

pâté, run a knife around the edge of each cup, release the pâté, and slide each onto serving dish. Serve with Low-Calorie Hollandaise Sauce. Makes 4 servings.

LOW-CALORIE HOLLANDAISE SAUCE

1 teaspoon lemon juice
2 tablespoons sweet butter
   or margarine, softened
Salt, dash red-pepper sauce

1 whole egg
1 egg white
2 tablespoons wine
   vinegar

Combine the egg, egg white and vinegar in the top of a double boiler over simmering water. Stirring vigorously with a whisk, cook over very low heat, until the mixture is thick and creamy. Remove from heat and beat in lemon juice and softened butter. Season to taste with salt, pepper sauce. Serve immediately. Makes about 1 cup.

NUTTED MERINGUE SHELL

4 egg whites
1 tablespoon lemon juice
   Pinch of salt
1½ tablespoons sugar
2 tablespoons dry skim
   milk

1 tablespoon Leroux
   Crème de Noya
2 tablespoons chopped
   toasted hazelnuts or
   almonds

Beat egg whites with lemon juice and salt until mixture forms soft peaks. Add sugar and dry milk solids, beating constantly until the mixture stands in firm peaks. Beat in Crème de Noya until very stiff. Fold in nuts. Shape meringue into a 10-inch round, on brown paper, piping sides into a 2-inch band. Bake at 200° F., a very low oven, about 2 hours, until dry. Turn off heat and let stand another 2 hours in warm oven to dry completely.

Berry Filling for Shell:

Wash and hull 4 cups fresh strawberries. Moisten with 3 tablespoons Leroux Raspberry Liqueur. Let stand in refrigerator, covered, for 3 hours. Spoon berries from liqueur into baked meringue shell. Blend liqueur with 1 cup fresh raspberries. Spoon over strawberries in shell. If desired, top with Crème Fraiche (below).

Creme Fraiche:

Combine ⅓ cup each heavy cream, yogurt, and sour cream. Stir smooth. Store in refrigerator.

LOW-CALORIE DESSERT CREPES

1¼ cups skim milk
2 egg whites
½ cup rice flour
½ cup all-purpose flour
¼ teaspoon salt

1 tablespoon sugar or substitute to equal
¼ teaspoon grated lemon rind
1 tablespoon peanut oil

Combine all ingredients except oil in blender or food processor and whirl until evenly blended. Let stand, covered, at least 1 hour before using. Warm oil in a 7-inch cast-iron skillet or crepe pan, add excess to the batter. Pour about 2 tablespoons batter into hot pan and tilt and turn the pan to spread the batter evenly. Let cook directly over the heat for about 30 seconds, until the top is dry and bottom lightly browned. Flip the crepe and brown the other side, about 15 seconds. Brush pan with oiled paper between crepes as necessary. Stack cooked crepes on a paper-lined tray. Makes about 15 to 16 crepes. Serve with Orange Sauce (recipe follows).

ORANGE SAUCE FOR CREPES

1 tablespoon sweet butter or margarine
2 sugar cubes Orange

2 tablespoons Leroux Cognac à l'Orange
2 tablespoons Seagram's Extra Dry Gin

At table, melt butter in flat chafing dish pan. Rub sugar cubes over orange skin and drop into pan. Let sugar begin to melt and caramelize, add Leroux Cognac à l'Orange and Seagram's Gin, a twist of the orange zest, and the juice of the orange. Stir to combine. Place crepes, one at a time, into hot sauce, fold over once, and then fold quickly into a triangle, like a handkerchief. As each crepe is folded, push it to the side of the pan. Makes about 8 low-calorie dessert servings.

DIETER AT THE BAR

In drinks, look to your mixers for quick cuts in calories. While there are variations in the calories of gin, vodka, rum, Scotch, Bourbon, Canadian, and blends, these differences are minor.

The alcohol portion of your spirits, whatever the source, is 7 calories per gram, 2 calories per gram fewer than fat, 3 more calories per gram than protein or carbohydrates. The remaining calorie differences come from the variation in the carbohydrate of liquors, wines, and liqueurs.

A far larger differential is found in mixers, between, let's say, a sweetened soda at about 85 calories, and a non calorie mixer such as water or club soda or mineral water, no-calorie soda, tea, or coffee, or for variety you might choose broth or diluted grapefruit juice. Would you be surprised to know that a 3½ ounce glass of many dry red or white wines totals about the same calories (as well as alcohol content) as a Scotch, gin or vodka drink made with 1 ounce of liquor and a non caloric mixer?

For extra eye appeal, and extra flavor, without calorie cost, garnish your lowered calorie drinks in style. Add a twist of lemon, a wedge of lime, a strawberry, or a mint sprig for drinks with more class than calories.

The most important diet tip—limit your drinks, as you limit your foods, in line with your calorie targets.

15

Have Party
Will Travel

You can pack up your party and take it to watch the game, or the sunset, or the stars, in backyard, picnic site, camp, or on a boat.

SOUR BAR IN A JUG

Combine in ½-gallon container, 1 bottle (750 milliliters) Seagram's 7 Crown, 12 ounces frozen lemonade concentrate, and 3 cups water. Cap and carry in a cooler.

SCOTTISH PASTIES

Make a sturdy pastry, as for 2-crust pie. Preheat skillet and brown 1 pound chopped meat, 1 diced onion. Stir in a beaten egg, handful of chopped parsley, season with salt, pepper, pinch dry mustard. Cool. Roll pastry, cut into 3- or 4-inch circles. Place 1 tablespoon meat filling in center of each round, fold over, press edges to seal. Brush tops with 1 egg beaten with 1 tablespoon water. Bake in 425° F. oven until golden brown, about 15 minutes. Cool and wrap.

SCOTTISH TRADITION

Serve the Scottish pasties (called "Cornish pies") with
The Glenlivet and water—branch water, at a clear brook.

MIXED-SALAD VEGETABLES

Combine your pick of vegetables, and toss with diced
onion, strips of cheese, olives, French dressing.

CANTALOUPE SURPRISE

Cut top off melon, remove seeds, fill with cubes of boiled
ham. Scoop out fruit for nibbling with ham.

SEAGRAM'S 7 SOUR CAKE

Prepare lemon frosting mix as directed, using Seagram's
7 Crown for liquid. Use to sandwich sliced pound cake.

CANADIAN COFFEE SIPPER

Pack instant coffee—espresso brew for deep flavor. Combine coffee and Seagram's V.O. in cup, sweeten to taste,
add hot water from a Thermos, top with whip cream
from a can.

MYERS'S HOT COCOA

Add ¾ cup Myers's Rum to one quart hot cocoa spiced
with a dash or two of cinnamon. Pour into a vacuum jug.

HOT BLOODY MARY

1 can (1 quart, 14 ounces) tomato juice
¼ cup lemon juice
1 teaspoon salt

¼ teaspoon ground cloves
Tabasco and Worcestershire sauce to taste
1 pint (500 milliliters) Wolfschmidt Vodka

Bring tomato juice, lemon juice, and seasonings to a simmer in a saucepan. Stir in vodka and pour into vacuum jug or jugs. Makes 2 quarts.

For hearty autumn appetites, bring along Scottish Pasties (recipe above) and an insulated jug of Scotch Baked Beans.

SCOTCH BAKED BEANS

6 strips bacon
2 cans (1 pound each) baked beans
1 teaspoon mustard
½ teaspoon ground ginger

¼ cup honey
2 tablespoons minced onion
¼ cup The Famous Grouse Scotch

Line a 2-quart bean pot with 4 of the bacon strips. Combine and add remaining ingredients. Top with remaining bacon; cover. Bake 1 hour at 325° F.; uncover during last 15 minutes.

16

How to Plan
a Big Bash

If you consider friends blessings, you may find yourself richer than you realized when you plan a big party. A holiday open house, a salute to a friend, a farewell to an old neighbor, or a welcome to a newly married pair may add up to a list of forty or fifty guests.

Your first key to success is to simplify and unclutter. Plan a menu of a few easy-to-prepare dishes, big enough to hold up through the evening, and set them out on a self-serve buffet. Include some special foods and some basics. Put a choice of punches on the buffet table, and the bar itself in another spot—separated for traffic.

PARTY STARTERS

A bright party setting, with colorful cloth and food, does part of the trick. Music sets the mood, but the best mixer of all is your own warmth as you greet guests at the door. Guide each to the bar and, drink in hand, to compatible conversation groups. Great parties take off with friendly person-to-person talk that's the best party game of all.

Let's look at four plans and their preparation:

1. CHEESE-TASTING BUFFET: Visit the best cheese shop in your area, or talk with the dairy manager of your supermarket, and advance-order an assortment of cheeses (see Chapter 10), including a large whole cheese, which you will partially cut at the start, and then use to replenish trays as the evening goes on.

Also order an assortment of breads and crackers to go with the cheeses—or better yet, bake your own breads.

2. HERO LOAVES: For an alternate plan, buy extra-long breads, assorted meats, cheese relishes, and prepare dramatic hero loaves cut to serve in sections.

3. PARTY PASTRIES: Prepare an assortment of finger-food savory pastries—strudel dough or phyllo leaves filled with Chicken Liver Paté, or zesty tuna mixture, or ricotta cheese and spinach beaten with egg and seasoned with nutmeg. Glaze your strudels with melted butter and bake in advance (possibly freeze) to reheat at party time. (See Chapter 9 for recipes.)

4. BUFFET SETUP: Or plan a buffet with two simply elegant dishes. Precook the sauce for shrimp curry in advance. Have the frozen shrimp cleaned, ready to be added before serving. Roast a large boneless beef round a day ahead, and it will be easier to slice cold.

SHRIMP CURRY FOR A CROWD

Peel 4 large onions and 4 cloves garlic. Clean 6 stalks celery. Core, peel, and quarter 4 tart apples, peel 4 ripe tomatoes. Chop all fine. Melt ¼ pound butter or margarine in large pan or Dutch oven. Add chopped mixture and 4 tablespoons or more curry powder, 1 tablespoon salt, 2 teaspoons pepper, ½ teaspoon nutmeg, ½ teaspoon ginger. Cook until vegetables are soft. Stir in ⅛ cup flour, add 2 quarts consommé, and simmer about 30 minutes. Sauce may be made ahead. Before serving, reheat sauce, add ½ cup Seagram's Extra Dry Gin, 6 pounds frozen cleaned shrimp. Bring to boil, simmer 5 minutes, until shrimp are pink and hot through. Serve with hot rice, bowls of curry accompaniments to which guests help themselves. Include shredded coconut, peanuts and raisins, chutney, kumquats, chopped green pepper or cucumber, toasted diced almonds. Makes 24 servings.

ROYAL ROAST BEEF

A great beef roast makes an elegant party, lordly feeling for the guests, and is easy on the host. A loin strip of beef is imposing (order it ahead, if necessary) and at 12 pounds it would provide enough thin beef slices to make about 48 servings. Roast at 300° F., about 16 minutes to the pound for rare meat, or until a meat thermometer roasted near the center registers 140° F. for rare, 160° F. for medium done. For extra flavor and tenderness, baste roast with Benchmark Sour Mash Premium Bourbon at start, then continue to baste with pan drippings.

Add a large rye bread or pumpernickel, sliced thinly, for easy sandwich assemblage.

Whatever your menu, plan on coffee or tea and a tray of cookies to signal the end of the party.

SCOTCH PUNCH BOWL

Pair roast beef simplicity with a punch that has special appeal to Scotch drinkers. Pour over ice block in punch bowl, 2 cans (6 ounces each) frozen lemonade concentrate. Add 2 bottles (750 ml. each) The Famous Grouse Scotch. Stir well to blend. Just before serving, add four large bottles club soda. Stir lightly. Serve over ice in Old-Fashioned glasses. Makes about 30 drinks.

In advance, empty 1 can (6 oz.) frozen lemonade concentrate in punch bowl. Add water as directed. Add 1 quart Seagram's 7 Crown. Stir well. Just before serving, add ice block and orange slice garnish. Add 1 quart club soda, stir gently. Makes 32 drinks.

17

Until the Next

UNTIL THE NEXT . . .

Make your farewells happy. Provide a place to linger for guests who need a little more time, and plan to serve coffee before guests are ready to depart. Make your own example one of "know your limits" . . . that's part of the plan for responsible hosting.

And when the party is over, thoughtful put-away is your best beginning for the next party. Clean glasses neatly stored, party supplies and equipment packed ready for next use, your bar replaced for day-to-day hospitality . . . the parties that just seem to happen, when you are prepared for them.

The good life is better when parties at your house are fun for the guests . . . and your own great pleasure.

Index

225

227

Drink Index

The recipes described in this book call for the use of the following brands:

Seagram's 7 Crown/American Whiskey/A Blend/80 Proof/Seagram Distillers Co., New York, N.Y.

Seagram's V.O./Imported Canadian Whisky/A Blend/86.8 Proof/Six Year Old/Seagram Distillers Co., New York, N.Y.

Seagram's Crown Royal/Imported in the Bottle/Blended Canadian Whisky/80 Proof/Seagram Distillers Co., New York, N.Y.

Seagram's Gin/Distilled from Grain/80 Proof/Seagram Distillers Co., New York, N.Y.

Wolfschmidt Vodka/Distilled from Grain/80 and 100 Proof/Seagram Distillers Co., New York, N.Y.

Benchmark Sour Mash Premium Bourbon/Bottled by The Old Benchmark Distilling Co., Louisville, Ky./86 Proof

The Glenlivet/Twelve Year Old/Unblended Scotch Whisky/86 Proof/The Glenlivet Distilling Co., New York, N.Y.

The Famous Grouse Blended Scotch Whisky/86 Proof/The Famous Grouse Import Co., New York, N.Y.

Myers's Rum/Imported and Bottled by Fred L. Myers's & Son Co., Baltimore, Md./80 Proof

Leroux/The Royal Family of International Liqueurs/General Wines and Spirits Co./54–70 Proof

Olmeca Tequila/Tequila, Jalisco, Mexico/80 Proof/La Fabrica La Martinena